BITS,

BYTES,

AND

BALANCE SHEETS

WALTER B. WRISTON, 1919–2005

BITS,

BYTES,

AND

BALANCE SHEETS

The New Economic

Rules of Engagement

in a Wireless World

by **Walter B. Wriston**
Former Chairman, Citicorp

HOOVER INSTITUTION PRESS | *Stanford University* | *Stanford, California www.hoover.org*

Hoover Institution Press Publication No. 557

Hoover Institution at Leland Stanford Junior University,
Stanford, California, 94305–6010

First printing 2007
14 13 12 11 10 09 08   9 8 7 6 5 4 3 2

Manufactured in the United States of America

The paper used in this publication meets the minimum
requirements of the American National Standard for
Information Sciences—Permanence of Paper for Printed
Library Materials, ANSI/NISO Z39.48–1992. ♾

Library of Congress Cataloging-in-Publication Data

Wriston, Walter B.
    Bits, bytes, and balance sheets : the new economic rules of
engagement in a wireless world / by Walter B. Wriston.
        p.   cm.— (Hoover institution press publication ; no. 557)
    Includes bibliographical references and index.
    ISBN-13: 978-0-8179-4861-0 (cloth : alk. paper)
    ISBN-10: 0-8179-4861-9 (cloth : alk. paper)
    1. Internet—Economic aspects.   2. Information technology.
3. Electronic commerce.   I. Title.
HC79.I55W74   2007
303.48'33—dc22   2007025485

For My Family—
Kathy, Cassy, Dick, Christopher, and Katy

CONTENTS

by *George P. Shultz*

Walter **Wriston** was a man of high intellect, and that made him comfortable in the world of ideas. He loved ideas—he enjoyed playing around with them, getting to know them, understanding their meaning. Walt also had immense energy and drive and a special kind of insight into the ways organizations operate. All of this made him comfortable in the world of work. That was something special because he could move from one world to the other. In the process, he could put the best of both together and find new insights into what the future holds. All of these unique characteristics are on display in this book, so here we have vintage Wriston, complete with a special lacing of wisdom and dry wit.

This is a book about the future as Walt saw it. He was confident but he also had his worries. He was as concerned about corporate excess as anyone, but was deeply dubious about the immense outpouring of rules designed to deal with it. Walt was a believer in those old-fashioned words "trust" and "character" and said, "A world without trust would be savage."

So this book begins with the idea that fundamentally you

count on a society of trustworthy people, but of course you don't leave it at that. Wriston quotes the late U.S. Supreme Court Justice Louis Brandeis, who said, "Sunshine is the best disinfectant." He also expects "honest law enforcement officers and effective auditors." Speaking of auditors, he uses that good old baseball phrase: "You can't hit what you can't see." Walt reminds me a little of Ronald Reagan quoting his favorite Midwest humorist, Mr. Dooley: "T-t-t-trust everybody, but c-c-c-cut the cards," or, in a phrase Reagan made famous with Mr. Gorbachev, "Trust but verify." Always on display is Walt's deep reverence for trust along with transparency—Brandeis's sunshine.

Walt's preoccupation, going back to his wonderful book *The Twilight of Sovereignty*, was with the information revolution and the meaning of that revolution. As he puts it, "Today the industrialists have been replaced by the masters of intellectual capital." That being the case, as Walt states in his own preface, "The new means of creating wealth produces, among other things, a new kind of economy. And, in turn, that new kind of economy requires new rules and new metrics because the old rules and metrics were crafted for another age."

The new age of intellectual capital and broadly available information requires a special kind of agility in differentiating the people and the organizations that have it from those who don't. Walt applies the phrase "the quick and the dead" to emphasize his point.

He was deeply disturbed about the inadequacy of our ways of measuring what is taking place. We measure the rate of savings as falling to zero at the same time as the net worth of Americans has never been so high and money is pouring into mutual funds. Walt worried about the expansion of what we call *services*, an expansion probably due to our not having a category in which to place important new developments, many of them associated with intellectual capital. I can re-member many conversations with Walt about this problem and we agreed on the importance of trying to change the way we describe our economy.

Consider this line of thinking: Our national accounts were created back in the 1920s and 1930s by some brilliant people at the National Bureau of Economic Research (NBER) who established categories to describe the economy of that era. Since then, our economy has changed dramatically. Many in-dustries that flourished in those earlier days no longer exist, and much of today's life is dominated by goods and services that were not even dreamt of back then.

We have kept the categories created by the NBER and what is the result? When new things come along, we try to fit them into those categories. But round pegs have an increasingly dif-ficult time fitting into square holes, and these days there are many oddly configured pegs for which no hole will do. In frus-tration, we call these new developments services, so we find ourselves in a progressively service-oriented economy. The ar-tificiality of our measurements means that our analytic capa-bilities are increasingly limited. We look at the numbers and try to estimate the total size of our economy or get a sense of its dynamism and productivity. But because our gauges are faulty, our analyses and judgments fall short.

Walt and I wondered what would happen if individuals pos-sessing the brilliance of those who created our national ac-counts eighty years ago were put to the task today, working from a clean sheet of paper. Would they create the accounts that we have today? Certainly not. They would be describing *today's* economy, and with these new kinds of numbers in hand, we would understand our economy much better.

Why not go back to the NBER and ask them to take on this task, including in their group high-powered statisticians drawn from those who do the current numbers and are familiar with all the problems of measurement? Two parallel measures, the old and the new, might be published for a period of time, and adaptations to the current system would likely develop. Our understanding of the dynamics of our economy would improve. Let's call this the "Wriston economy"—an economy in which Walt's brilliance and insight inform what is going on today and what is likely to happen in the future.

In this book, Walt Wriston gives us ideas to use, insights into what the future holds, and suggestions as to what can be done to best achieve a bright and promising future. Then, just as Walt always did, we can enjoy that future even as it is unfolding.

George P. Shultz
July 2007

A native of New York, Mr. Shultz graduated from Princeton University in 1942. After serving in the Marine Corps (1942–45), he earned a Ph.D. at MIT. Mr. Shultz taught at MIT and The University of Chicago Graduate School of Business, of which he became dean in 1962. He was appointed secretary of labor in 1969, director of the Office of Management and Budget in 1970, and secretary of the treasury in 1972. From 1974 to 1982, he was president of Bechtel Group, Inc. Mr. Shultz served in the Reagan administration as chairman of the President's Economic Policy Advisory Board (1981–82) and secretary of state (1982–89). He is chairman of the J.P. Morgan Chase International Council. Since 1989, he has been a Distinguished Fellow at the Hoover Institution, Stanford University.

A NOTE TO READERS

The chapters in this book were written over a period of years and were adapted from speeches and articles by Mr. Wriston. Throughout the book, there are occasional references to time ("today," "these days"), so the reader will want to know the dates on which particular chapters were written. In a few places, Mr. Wriston makes predictions that have now come to pass. These instances are cited in the accompanying footnotes. Listed below are the dates of the speeches and articles on which the chapters are based.

Chapter 1   **Unintended Consequences**
            Part 1: Based on article "Laws," September 26, 2002
            Part 2: (from heading "Not Immediately Recognized" to end): Based on speech "The Technology of Freedom," given at the Mt. Pelerin Society meeting in Vancouver, British Columbia, Canada, August 29, 1999

Chapter 2   **The Creation of Wealth**
            Based on speech given at the Arthur Andersen Conference in Chicago, June 1, 1994

Chapter 3   **Bits, Bytes, Power, and Diplomacy**
            Based on speech "Bits, Bytes, Power, and Diplomacy,"

given at the U.S. Institute of Peace, Washington, D.C.,
April 1, 1997

Chapter 4 New Rules: Different in Kind, Not Degree
Based on speech "Shadow and Reality: The Quick and
the Dead," given at the Fortune Financial Services
Technology Forum, March 4, 1999

Chapter 5 The Whiskey Ain't Working Anymore
Based on speech "The Whiskey Ain't Working
Anymore," given at Perspectives '95, Philadelphia,
September 14, 1995

Chapter 6 What Gets Measured, Gets Done
Based on speech "The Great Disconnect," given at the
Ernst & Young Cap Gemini Conference, Boston,
October 2, 2000

**Chapter 7 The Great Disconnect: Balance Sheets Versus
Market Value**
Based on speech "The Great Disconnect," given at the
Ernst & Young Cap Gemini Conference, Boston,
October 2, 2000

Chapter 8 Politically Correct Versus Accurate Earnings
Based on unpublished article "Politically Correct
Versus Accurate Earnings," August 7, 2002

Chapter 9 Global Accounting for a Global Market
Based on article "The Solution to Scandals? Simpler
Rules," *Wall Street Journal*, August 5, 2002

Chapter 10 Other People's Money
Based on "Other People's Money," an online article
written for PR Newswire and posted at Disclosure
Resource.com, July 11, 2002. Another version of this
chapter's content appeared as "A Code of Our Own"
in the *Wall Street Journal* on January 16, 2003.

PREFACE

A Momentous Revolution

When my book *The Twilight of Sovereignty* was published in 1992 by Simon & Schuster, it attempted to explain—to our business and political leaders especially—how technology was transforming our world. Many of these leaders heard the book's message, but only in a kind of detached sense, as they did not relate it to their own personal or corporate situation.

As the years went by, however, and the trends revealed in *The Twilight of Sovereignty* grew more and more visible, it became clear that we are, in fact, living through a true and momentous revolution, one that is affecting all aspects of our lives.

The Internet has changed everything. No one knows for certain how many people are connected to it; in fact, any estimate is out of date the day it is announced. This evolving situation makes, and will continue to make, a huge difference to the very nature of the nation-state. It is altering the way institutions, both public and private, are managed and the way individuals react to each other, their workplaces, and their governments. And the race to win economically is between those who "get it" and those who don't; in other words, it is between "the quick and the dead."

To "get it" means more than just having a personal computer on your desk or going to conferences with PowerPoint presentations. It is a mind-set. It is knowing that, for the first time in history, our economy is truly global—even though some areas are currently left out—and that the products we are making or the services we are rendering can suddenly show up in this new marketplace supplied by a firm we've never heard of, from a place we have difficulty finding on the map. The competitors we've known in the past may be around the corner, but the new ones can be anywhere on the globe. This is a dynamic situation beyond anything we have known, and it will only get more dynamic as time goes on.

Examples abound of once very successful companies that failed to change their ways in the light of new circumstances or failed to change them quickly enough to save themselves. For example, steel was, by any measure, the basic industry of the industrial age, but the huge steel companies were slow to appreciate the threat of the mini-mills, whose new technology allowed them to produce steel at a cost per ton that was about 20 percent lower than that of the big integrated mills. Although the big steel companies invested billions of dollars in new technology, not one of them introduced mini-mill technology into its own product mix until it was too late.

This story of too little, too late—or, more accurately, of the quick and the dead—has been repeated over and over, in industry after industry. Indeed, of all the companies in the original Dow Jones Industrial Average first published in 1896, only one, General Electric, still enjoys that position. In some cases, not only did the company disappear, but also the industry it served faded away.

Although all of the factors described in *The Twilight of Sovereignty* are now operating at flank speed, the main driver of the revolutionary social changes we are experiencing today is the transforming way in which wealth is created. Just as the landed gentry gave way to the industrialists as the Industrial Revolution gained momentum, so today the industrialists have been replaced by the masters of intellectual capital (see chapter 2).

Whenever changes of this magnitude take place, every facet of society is affected because the new means of creating wealth produces, among other things, a new kind of economy. And, in turn, that new kind of economy requires new rules and new metrics because the old rules and metrics were crafted for another age.

This does not mean that basics such as "two plus two is four" have now gone by the boards, but it does mean that in the new economy, in which intellectual capital is more important than physical capital, some of the old rules have diminished in significance and some new ones have gained strength.

The purpose of this book, a follow-up to *The Twilight of Sovereignty*, is to lay out some of the consequences of the changes produced by the new economy, to define the new rules, and to explore some of the promising initiatives under way to create a system of measuring and valuating assets that reflects not yesterday's reality but the quick and the dead economic reality of today.

Walter B. Wriston

Unintended Consequences

The law of unintended consequences was at work with the passage of the Sarbanes-Oxley bill in 2002. This bill, which was ostensibly designed to help prevent cases of corporate malfeasance, now joins the approximately 300 other laws targeted at the same problem that attempt to turn moral questions into legal issues. The overregulation that surely will result is partly the fault of business itself because practices that are often overlooked in boom times may, in lean times, appear to be egregious excesses that never should have been allowed to happen.

The twenty-four-hour news cycle drums into the American consciousness the realization that something is amiss. At some point, the public demands that the government "do something" and Congress responds. But laws written in the heat of the moment rarely achieve their stated purpose and often have perverse effects. Sarbanes-Oxley, like many laws before it, delegates to a regulator the ability to write the regulations that presumably protect a "public interest" that generations of lawyers and philosophers have labored for years to define, with mixed results. With the passage of time, the regulators produce a plethora of regulations that have the force of law, and an administrative judge—often from the same regulatory body—becomes prosecutor, judge, and jury. Inevitably, the regulator substitutes his or her judgment for that of the market, and the system becomes backward-looking at a time when worldwide competition requires forward-looking innovation to survive. The system becomes neither consumer oriented nor business oriented, but *bureaucracy* oriented. In the banking sector, for years the regulators held below market the interest rate that banks could pay to consumers. That regulation cheated the public out of a fair return on its money but satisfied the bureaucracy. It took years and an act of Congress to get rid of it.

Long ago, John Locke warned against the delegation of authority to nonelected regulators who claim to represent the public interest. Locke said that the legislature cannot transfer the power of making laws to any other hands because it is a power delegated by the people, and they to whom it is delegated cannot pass it over to others.[1] But passing it on to others is just what Congress does; the evidence is found in the thousands of pages of the *Federal Register*. As the regulations proliferate, able people who make the economy run will seek other employment. To the coming thicket of regulations is now added the congressional reciprocal gift to the plaintiffs' bar, which will add untold cost to American companies and do nothing for productivity. To ask how we can regulate instead of how we can improve is to demolish our competitive

---

1. John Locke, *Two Treatises of Government*, 1689, ed. Peter Laslett (Cambridge: Cambridge University Press, 1960), 380–81.

position in the world and, more important, to destroy our wealth.

In our system, the board of directors has the responsibility to hire and fire the CEO and to monitor the operations of the corporation. A director has great responsibility but no operating authority, and this equation requires men and women of judgment and experience who are, by definition, busy people. The concept embedded in the new law of either having a "financial expert" on the audit committee or publishing the reason for not having such an individual onboard sounds intelligent, but what is the definition of such an expert?

The Securities and Exchange Commission (SEC), acting on Sarbanes-Oxley guidelines, must furnish the official profile of a "financial expert." (By any definition, Enron had such a person on its audit committee.) But if he or she is lied to or if information is withheld, the most skilled person in the world will be of no avail. And if one "expert," as defined by a bureaucracy, is appointed, does he or she have an increased duty of care? Who would want the job?

If the balance between reward and liability, now barely tolerable, is weighted by the new law toward the liability end, directors of worth will become increasingly hard to find. In Tom Wolfe's novel *The Bonfire of the Vanities*, when the hapless central character, Sherman McCoy, is asked by a reporter on the steps of the courthouse what his occupation is, he replies, "professional defendant." No one wants to list such a title as his or her occupation, so if regulations continue to point in that direction, it will become difficult, if not impossible, to get anyone of substance to serve on a board of directors. And so, at the end of the day, the law designed in good faith to

protect the public may in fact have the unintended conse-
quence of lowering the quality of corporate governance.

Not Immediately Recognized

In her book *A Distant Mirror*, the great historian Barbara
Tuchman tells us of the unintended consequences to society
of the invention of the chimney: "As distinct from a hole in
the roof, these chimneys were a technological advance of the
eleventh century . . . that by warming individual rooms,
brought lords and ladies out of the common hall where all had
once eaten together and gathered for warmth, separating the
owners from the retainers. No other invention brought more
comfort and refinement, although at the cost of a widening
social gulf."[2] In short, Tuchman is saying that the lowly chimney not only made privacy possible, but it also engendered all
of the societal changes that flowed from that concept.

A little more complicated than a chimney was the forerunner of the modern air conditioner that Jacob Perkins put together in 1834 using a coil, a condenser, a fan, and a motor.
It was an invention that changed not only American politics
but also the industrial map of the world. Here's how.

In the early history of the United States, Alexander Hamilton made a political trade in order to assure the passage of our
Constitution. In exchange for having the federal government
assume the debts of the states, the nation's capital was to
move from New York to Washington, D.C., with a stop in

---

2. Barbara W. Tuchman, *A Distant Mirror: The Calamitous 14th Century*
(New York: Alfred A. Knopf, 1978), 12.

Philadelphia. Then, as now, Washington was almost unlivable in the summer months; indeed, to escape the heat and humidity, President Jefferson moved to Monticello for two months each summer and Congress adjourned. Today, air conditioning allows our government to operate 365 days a year. Whatever one may think of this, few would deny that it has had a profound effect on the very nature of our government. Air conditioning has also made it possible to turn many tropical lands into economic powerhouses.

And finally, there is the automobile. Its invention ended the isolation of the family farm as the youths of the day used cars to go to town, get away from their parents, and create their own privacy in thousands of automobile backseats.

None of the consequences of these technological advances was immediately recognized.

New Forms of Business

Just as the advent of the automobile spawned many new industries, from the corner garage to body shops to gas stations, so the new economy has triggered new forms of business. One of the most interesting is the incubator.

Although the form and size of incubators differ from place to place, they basically consist of a group of computer-literate consultants who, instead of going to a business dressed in their blue suits and carrying bulging briefcases, have the business come to them.

The workspace is designed to encourage the sharing of information. There are no private offices, only desks in an open space, although there are plenty of conference rooms if privacy with a client is desired. Everything is designed to attract the most competent people. The dress code is simply what people happen to be wearing. There is a common space—the modern equivalent of the water cooler—where employees gather to take a break and share the latest idea. These spaces are often equipped with video games, pool tables, and kitchens stocked with all manner of food and soft drinks. The coffee is always on, and the men's room is stocked with razors and shaving cream in the event that someone has to work all night.

Unlike most consulting companies, where people tend to specialize in, say, retail or financial services, in the new incubator model, men and women become generalists about how to get a business under way. A team of people sets up shop to incubate a new business in a dedicated open workspace that is furnished with a staff, computers, paper, pencils, sound Internet connections, and a Rolodex containing the names of specialists on everything from patent protection to human resources. The team literally takes an idea from a dream to a business, and when it is formed enough to survive by itself, it is moved out to its own quarters. The incubator is then ready for another startup that is in need of everything but a great idea.

As far as I know, this is a brand-new thing under the sun. The incubator furnishes startups with the infrastructure that, whether through lack of experience or money or both, they are unable to obtain acting alone.

The new economy has very low barriers, if any, to entry. In times past, one had to have capital, sometimes in large amounts, to start a business. The idea of going up against the giants of the industry was unheard of. Today, a person with a killer idea and a maxed-out credit card can challenge the largest company. Of course, not all such attempts are successful, but enough home runs are being hit to keep the entrepreneurs steadily coming on. Someone is always out there with the next "new thing," so no business can coast along without a worry. The staffs of the incubators are encouraged to engage in constant learning, which is the touchstone of the new economy and the only road to survival in this changing environment.

We can argue about whether all of these advances, and their unintended consequences, have been good or bad for the human race. But either way, one thing is undeniable: they have had a profound effect on the way the world works.

A World Connected

The radio, then television, and now the Internet have tied the peoples of the world together in ways never before seen or even imagined.

This marriage of the computer and telecommunications to create a global information/network economy has touched a great many aspects of our lives, not the least of which are the relationships of one government to another, of citizen to government, and of nationalized industries to the private sector.

When great transitions like this occur in the world, there is often no clear dividing line between the ascendancy of the new and the decline of the old. For example, the dawn of the industrial age, which is often dated from James Watt's design of the steam engine in 1776, did not mean that agriculture suddenly vanished from the face of the earth. On the contrary, farms in the United States continued to produce more and more with fewer and fewer people while output in relative terms declined against industrial production.

The industrial age in which most of us grew up is now slowly fading into the information/network society, and as much as some may wish to do so, we can't go back again. The information age exists and it will not go away. Indeed, it will only move faster and become more pervasive.

In the United States, thousands of manufacturing jobs that were once a mainstay of our society are never going to come back, nor will we ever again see American farms employing the approximately 20 million people who worked on them at the beginning of the twentieth century.

This does not mean that manufacturing as we know it will cease to exist any more than farming disappeared with the rise of industry. But it does mean that for a huge and growing sector of society there is, in fact, a new economy that is as different from the industrial economy as the industrial economy was from the agricultural.

Although sea changes have always been a part of life on this planet, the current velocity of today's technology-driven change has no historical precedent. The period between novel and obsolete gets shorter and shorter.

For example, it took forty years for radio to draw 50 million listeners in the United States, and it took thirteen years for television to gain a like number. But it took only four years for the Worldwide Web to attract 50 million users in the United States alone, and access to the Web is growing exponentially.

Today, the extent to which technology has influenced us and infiltrated every aspect of our lives is unprecedented. One has only to reflect on the hype about the Y2K problem. We were told, on the one hand, that it would cause a worldwide depression and that we should stockpile food and water, as the power grid would go down and all the lights would go out. On the other hand were those "experts" who predicted only minor inconvenience.

As it turned out, the "experts" were right. But the point is not who was proven right or wrong. Rather, it is that microchip technology has become imbedded in so many things, from the locks on our cars to the air conditioning systems in our homes, that our lives are inexorably intertwined with technology as never before.

The massive upheaval in the former Soviet Union is another good illustration of how potent this link has become. Although governments maintain elaborate intelligence-gathering facilities, when a crisis arises, eyes in all countries now turn to the television set, which has become standard furniture in all government crisis-management offices, and everyone tunes in to one of the twenty-four-hour cable news networks, such as CNN.

The foreign minister of the former Soviet Union, Eduard Shevardnadze, put it this way during the Yeltsin coup: "Praise be information technology! Praise be CNN. . . . Anyone who owned a parabolic antenna able to see this network's transmissions had a complete picture of what was happening."[3]

That such a statement could ever have come from a senior officer of what used to be a closed and secretive society would have been unthinkable just a decade earlier. Shevardnadze was right. The only ones in Moscow during the Yeltsin coup who did not know what was going on were the people in the U.S. Embassy, which did not have CNN.

Although historians are rarely able to identify the roots of a sea change while living through it, we can identify the sources of today's sea change with a remarkable degree of accuracy. They can be pinpointed to the U.S. Congress's passage of the GI Bill of Rights after World War II.

The GI bill made a college education possible for many returning servicemen and women who probably would not otherwise have had that opportunity. It was the last big government program that worked. Despite the fact that the returning service personnel were given what amounted to a voucher good at any college, no one raised the church-and-state issue that is part of the current conversation about vouchers in public schools. The veterans could, and did, go to public colleges and universities, including any religious school of their choice. All of our colleges and universities had to vie for these students, and competition had its usual result: a better product. It can be argued that open competition helped to make many American colleges and universities world-class institutions. The flow of graduates from this huge program helped position the United States to lead the information/network economy.

---

3. Eduard A. Shevardnadze, *The Future Belongs to Freedom* (New York: The Free Press, 1991), 207.

The significance of the GI bill and its unintended consequences has not been lost on the people of what used to be called the Third World, now more appropriately referred to as "developing countries." Today, more than half of all college graduates are from developing countries; indeed, Mexico has more graduate engineers than France, and India more than all of Europe. As the year 2000 arrived, it was estimated that students from the developing nations made up three-fifths of all university students.[4]

The message is that economic progress is largely a process of increasing the relative contribution of knowledge. And that message has finally gotten through to large segments of the world.

Knowledge Is Power

Not only are massive historical transitions disruptive, even often painful, but they also upset long-held beliefs and require us to think anew—which in itself is a painful process. We have to change the way we think of our jobs, our governments, our relationships, and, indeed, the way the world works. It is often easier to ignore changes and stick to what worked in the past than to sail into uncharted waters. But the new reality is that old solutions will not yield answers to new problems.

From the beginning of time, power has been based on knowledge. Someone learned to use a burning-glass to start a fire. Someone was able to find out where enemy troops were.

---

4. William B. Johnston, "Global Work Force 2000: The New World Labor Market," *Harvard Business Review* (March–April 1991): 119.

Someone knew how to build a castle wall strong enough to withstand a siege until someone else learned how to build a catapult or cannon to penetrate that wall. Some politician found a pollster who gave notice of what the citizens really worried about. Timely information has always conferred power in both the commercial and the political marketplaces.

The history of the world is strewn with wonderful inventions, but most were designed to solve specific problems: wheels to move things, engines of all kinds to supply power, and clocks and compasses to tell time and direction. But the inventions that made possible the information revolution of today were of a very different sort. They changed the way we solve problems.

For example, when Johann Gutenberg pioneered movable-type printing in Europe circa 1438 and when the group at Intel designed the integrated circuit in the 1970s, the way we record, store, access, and peruse knowledge made quantum leaps forward—leaps that affected not only how we do our jobs but also what we do.

These two events are just as important as they sound. In modern terms, Gutenberg broke the monopoly of the monks who copied manuscripts by hand and jealously guarded them. The monks understood with great clarity that knowledge is power and thus should not be dispensed lightly. In fact, in some places, the books were chained to the shelves.

Contrast that mind-set with the fact that today a researcher sitting anywhere in the world with a computer and a modem can tap into the databases of the Library of Congress, the Bibliothèque Nationale de France, and the British Library or search the catalogs of thousands of other libraries around the world.

The decentralization of data today is proceeding at incredible speed. As *Forbes* magazine's Rich Karlgaard has pointed out: "In 1977, 99 percent of the world's computing power resided on mainframes and minicomputers. . . . By 1992 the percentages had flipped: 99 percent of computing power sat collectively on the world's desktop (and laptop) computers."[5]

The effect of this has been that knowledge, which at one time was a kind of ornament for the rich and powerful, is now increasing our ability to manipulate matter and thereby generate new substances and products unhinted at in nature and undreamed of only a few years ago.

The signs are unmistakable: the explosion of knowledge caused by the information revolution, combined with the speed with which it is transferred across what were once defended sovereign borders, is having a drastic and far-reaching impact on the way the world works.

This is not because computer operators have replaced clerk typists. It is because the human struggle to survive and to prosper now depends on our ability to develop a new understanding of what constitutes wealth.

---

5. Rich Karlgaard, "Editor's Letter," *Forbes ASAP* (January 1994): 9.

CHAPTER 2

The Creation of Wealth

Over the years, wealth—and the perception of what constitutes it—has changed dramatically. But one thing remains constant and certain: when the *means* by which wealth is created changes, the whole structure of a society and its economy changes with it. Then conflict usually follows as the old rich understandably try to hang onto what made them wealthy and deplore the *nouveaux riches* for trying to assume power that the old rich believe rightfully belongs to them alone.

Virtually every society in history has believed that wealth flows mainly from one form of capital, from one type of productive activity, or from one particular sector of society. However, societies have often been wrong about their source of wealth, causing misery to themselves and others.

Right or wrong, however, both a society's beliefs about its source of wealth and the underlying reality of that source crucially affect political and social structures and the allocation of power.

Forms of Wealth

What *is* wealth? How is it generated, used, and saved?

For thousands of years, men were nomads who attached themselves to herds of animals moving from pasture to pasture. Wealth was counted in the size of the herd. Men owned nothing that could not be carried on their backs or the backs of their animals. Land was not regarded as a form of wealth, and its permanent control formed no part of the scanty political institutions of the day.

When village agriculture began to appear, land began to be seen as a form of wealth, as did water. Men started to lay down rules about the ownership of land and about water rights, and political power shifted away from nomadic chieftains and toward territorial rulers. The ownership and control of land and, later, of the natural resources the land contained translated into wealth and political authority.

As men learned to use power other than that of animals, the world started to change again. For example, in 1781, Richard Arkwright's water-powered cotton factory opened for business, ushering in a whole new era. Seven years later, a steam-powered plant commenced operation. This was followed by the steamship, the loom, the locomotive, and the invention of the production line that shifted the perception of what constituted wealth away from the ownership of land and toward industrial production. This process did not occur overnight, and indeed, like most change, it was not well received at the time, as all change threatens power structures.

With the twenty-first century now under way, it has become popular among some businesspeople to say that real wealth comes only from industry because industry produces things we can handle, things that are machined and solid, things that we can see and touch. Thus, we are told by these businesspeople, only manufacturing creates *real value* by producing *real goods* for sale. Yet manufacturing itself was seen in an unfavorable light only a few hundred years ago.

The tendency to focus on one means of producing wealth to the exclusion of all others is not a new phenomenon. In the early days of our republic, Benjamin Franklin noted, "Agriculture is truly productive of new wealth; manufacturers only change forms, and whatever value they give to the material they work upon, they in the meantime consume an equal value in provisions."[1] Speaking in today's parlance, what Franklin was saying is that, even then, manufacturing was seen by some people, including himself, as a zero-sum game.

Today, the information/network revolution has changed the very source of wealth from material to information—knowledge applied to work to create value. And just as the invention and use of mechanical sources of power changed over time, so the perception of how wealth is created, the invention of the microchip, and the global telecom network are rapidly changing just about everything we do today, as well as how we do it.

Pursuit of Information

It is now hard to find a product—from an automobile to a telephone—that is not dependent in some way on the mi-

---

1. Letter from Benjamin Franklin to Cadwalader Evans, written in 1767, reprinted from Samuel Hazard, ed., *Hazard's Register of Pennsylvania* XVI, no. 5 (August 1, 1835), 66.

crochip. Everyone knows that all the lights would go out, all the airplanes would stop flying, and all the financial institutions and many of the factories would shut down if the computer software that runs their systems suddenly disappeared. And most of the machinery would grind to a halt if the software that controls it failed. Indeed, the machines that produce things and the computers that control them are now so intertwined that there is no meaningful line between manufacturing and service anymore.

Since only about 2 percent of a microchip is material cost, material resources are no longer very important as sources of wealth. What has happened is that we are producing more and more with less and less labor. To that extent, industry mirrors what happened to farming. We used to have 20 million farmers in America; now we have fewer than 2 million, yet we feed ourselves and many others around the world.

Now the pursuit of wealth is largely the pursuit of information and the application of information to the means of production. When we apply knowledge to ongoing tasks, we increase productivity. And when we apply it to new tasks, we create innovation. Thus, competition for the best information is vastly different from yesteryear's rivalry for the best rubber plantations and the best coalfields. And companies and nations that compete for information are becoming very different from those that once competed primarily for territory and material resources.

The new economic powerhouses are masters not of huge material resources but of ideas and technology. Singapore and Hong Kong, two Asian tigers, demonstrate the growing irrelevance of territory in weighing wealth and power. This shift affects not only nations but also individual businesses.

The proliferation of information technology, ranging from the telephone to the fax machine to fiber-optic cables, has flooded the world with data moving at nearly the speed of light to all regions of the globe.

This does not mean just more of the same. For thousands of years, news could travel only as fast as a horse could run or a ship could sail. Military power was similarly impeded. Indeed, Napoleon's armies could move no faster than those of Julius Caesar.

Today, all that has changed. Writing in the foreword to the Rand study "Preparing for Conflict in the Information Age," Alvin and Heidi Toffler observed, "The way any society engages in conflict reflects the way it does a lot of other things— especially the way its economy is organized. Just as the invention of paper made possible the preparation and transmission of complex orders, so also did it change organizations by permitting the mobilization of large forces through the delegation of authority."[2]

The Rand study suggests that information is no longer in a subsidiary position but "is now being moved into a transcendent, if not independent role."[3] The study goes on to say: "Information should now be considered and developed as a distinct fourth dimension of national power."[4] This conclusion is a far cry from traditional military doctrine.

---

2. Alvin and Heidi Toffler, in foreword to *In Athena's Camp: Preparing for Conflict in the Information Age*, by John Arquilla and David Ronfeldt (Santa Monica, CA: Rand, 1997).

3. John Arquilla and David Ronfeldt, *In Athena's Camp: Preparing for Conflict in the Information Age* (Santa Monica, CA: Rand, 1997), 418–419.

4. Ibid.

Today, the minicam is omnipresent, but in the late eighteenth century there were no photographs of George Washington or Thomas Jefferson. Great national leaders were almost anonymous to all but those who had seen them in person. The czar of Russia traveled unrecognized throughout Europe. The ability of a sovereign to keep information secret, and thus maintain a tight grip on power, began to erode with the invention of the paved road, the optical telegraph, and the newspaper. Gossip in the coffee houses was replaced by newspapers, and, as Richard Brown has noted, "The society in which politics operated shifted from a communal discipline to a market-oriented competitive regimen in which the foundation of influence changed."[5]

Government viewed all of these developments with a wary eye. In 1835, Emperor Francis I of Austria turned down a request for permission to build a steam railroad lest it carry revolution to his throne. His intuition was more acute than he realized.

Years later, with the advent of the telephone, another sovereign saw danger in a new technology. Leon Trotsky reportedly proposed to Joseph Stalin that a modern telephone system be built in the new Soviet state. Stalin brushed off the idea, saying that he could imagine no greater instrument of counterrevolution in his time. What would he have thought if he had lived to see the Yeltsin coup, which utilized Relcom, an independent computer network that linked Moscow with eighty other Soviet cities and was plugged into similar net-

---

5. Richard D. Brown, *Knowledge Is Power: The Diffusion of Information in Early America, 1700–1865* (New York: Oxford University Press, 1989), 279.

works in Europe and the United States to spread the news of the coup? Even more ironic was that after the KGB blocked many trunk lines, Yeltsin communicated with his greatest ally, Mayor Sobchak of St. Petersburg, via the government's own telephone network. This stands in sharp contrast to the fact that in 1917 it took four to six weeks for the news of Czar Nicholas's abdication to reach the people of pre-Soviet Russia.

In America, each new administration comes into office with an agenda, and the initial 7 A.M. staff meetings in the Roosevelt Room are full of optimism. After a month or two, the meetings open with, "Did you see what the *Post* said this morning?" or "Did you hear what Brian Williams said last night?" followed by "What is our response?"

As President John F. Kennedy once remarked, "The Ship of State is the only one that leaks from the top." Although one can and should argue whether this is good or bad for public policy, it is, in the early twenty-first century, quite simply a reality.

Particle Finance

The changing perception of what constitutes wealth poses huge problems in expanding or even maintaining the power of government. Unlike land or industrial plants, information resources are not bound to a particular geography, nor are they easily taxed and controlled by governments. In an economy dominated by products that consist largely of information, governmental power erodes rapidly.

As *Forbes* magazine contributing editor George Gilder wrote some years ago: "A steel mill [the exemplary industry of the industrial age] lends itself to control by governments. Its massive output is easily measured and regulated at every point by government. By contrast, the typical means of production of the new epoch is a man at a computer workstation, designing microchips comparable in complexity to the entire steel facility, to be manufactured from software programs comprising a coded sequence of electronic pulses that can elude every export control and run a production line anywhere on the globe."[6]

What Gilder was saying is that today, a person like Microsoft chairman Bill Gates, who has the skills to write and market a complex software system that can produce a billion dollars of revenue, can walk past any customs officer in the world with this software in his head or stuffed in his pocket and have "nothing of value" to declare.

Dartmouth professor James Brian Quinn's book *Intelligent Enterprise* brilliantly analyzes what a knowledge-based business must do to keep out of the corporate graveyard in this new electronic economy where the source of wealth is information.[7] It has to change the way it does just about everything.

The shift to the new economy has given new prominence to what John Maynard Keynes called the "symbol" economy as opposed to the "real" economy.[8] This shift assigns new

---

6. George Gilder, "The Emancipation of the CEO," *Chief Executive* (January–February 1988): 9.

7. James Brian Quinn, *Intelligent Enterprise: A Knowledge and Service Based Paradigm for Industry* (New York: The Free Press, 1992).

8. Peter F. Drucker, "Keynes: Economics as a Magical System," *Virginia Quarterly Review* 22 (1946): 534.

meaning to the old terms "earned income" and "unearned income."

The old idea was that the idle rich collected interest and dividends on invested capital while doing nothing to produce that income. Indeed, "coupon clipping" was perceived as a term of opprobrium. On the other hand, wages, tips, and commissions were earned by the sweat of one's brow and were thus seen as the fruits of honest labor. The implication was that earned income was good, and unearned income bad. With the advent of the information/network economy, the balance between earned and unearned income began to shift as an increasing number of Americans became knowledge workers who invested their money in the market instead of savings accounts.

Although numbers vary, by late 1999, the *Wall Street Journal* reported that 52 percent of American families owned securities. In 1997, Internal Revenue Service figures showed that for every dollar of earned income, the worker was getting about $0.25 in interest and dividends. By the turn of the century, various tax-deferred vehicles had been crafted by Congress and were rapidly filling up with cash. The capital gains in these vehicles were uncounted in the IRS numbers and must have been huge by 1999 because of the long bull market.

The social effect of all this was the creation of what has been called the "investor class." Over time, this class will become a political force as its members are interested in preserving their financial assets from confiscatory taxes and oppressive regulations that stifle innovation. Although Claremont Graduate University social science professor and business thinker Peter Drucker long predicted what he called "pension fund socialism,"[9] which indeed has arrived, a more recent trend is toward the individual's personal control of his or her financial wealth. Wealth is being created not by making and selling things, although this is still a large part of the economy, but by taking, trading, and managing risk in the financial sector. Because every asset carries some risk, the market creates ways to lay off the risks we don't want or can't bear to an insurance company or by the use of some financial derivatives. The idea of breaking down every risk into smaller and smaller parts was given the name "particle finance,"[10] and modem technology is giving us the means to do so. The idea is to find the most efficient balance between risk and return. Charles Sanford, who did some of the pioneering work on particle finance, put it this way:

"Risk management is the process of moving clients closer to their desired risk profiles by helping them shed unwanted risks or acquire new risks that suit their portfolios. At times, this can be done simply by matching a client who wants to shed a risk with one who wants to acquire that risk. More often, it involves unbundling, transforming, and repackaging risks into bundles tailored to fit the particular needs of various clients."[11]

Many of the ways to manage risk turned out to be less than perfect and sometimes gave a false sense of security. But as

---

9. Peter F. Drucker, *The Unseen Revolution: How Pension Fund Socialism Came to America* (New York: HarperCollins, 1976), 1.

10. Charles S. Sanford, Jr., "Financial Markets in 2020" (paper presented at the Federal Reserve Bank of Kansas City's Symposium on "Changing Capital Markets: Implications for Monetary Policy," Jackson Hole, WY, August 20, 1993).

11. Ibid.

failures were assessed, new plans were devised to correct past errors in the same manner that various safety devices were installed on machines in the wake of accidents. And the process continues. Indeed, the creation of all these new risk-sharing techniques has produced a whole new cottage industry. Hardly any of these derivatives would be possible without the power of the computer.

Government has no such text to look to, but it will also have to learn what it can and cannot do with a subsequent effect on the way business operates.

In his great historical work *The Wheels of Commerce*, Fernand Braudel wrote that the sovereign's first task has always been to "secure obedience, to gain for itself the monopoly of the use of force in a given society, neutralizing all the possible challenges inside it and replacing them with what Max Weber called 'legitimate violence.'"[12]

In the Middle Ages, the central government took over the private armies of the feudal lords and the city-states to create that monopoly of power. Today, with such acts of domestic terrorism as the World Trade Center attack of September 11, 2001, our government has found that we are once again facing new private armies, not loyal to feudal lords but composed of terrorists controlled by small countries or factions within countries. Clearly, the modern terrorist understands information technology and its uses.

Whatever one's views of the matter, few would doubt that this presents difficult dilemmas for governments. Some prob-

12. Fernand Braudel, *The Wheels of Commerce: Civilization and Capitalism, 15th–18th Century*, vol. 2 (New York: Harper & Row, 1982), 515.

lems are just too big for any one country to handle, and terrorism is one of them.

Long ago, sovereigns in many different countries came to the same conclusion about piracy and banded together to outlaw the practice. Slavery is another case in point. The first significant international agreement to abolish the practice was reached in 1885 at the Berlin Conference, which was followed in 1890 by the Brussels Act, signed by eighteen countries. The security of our modern states may require similar joint treaties to outlaw terrorism.

As the concept and reality of the importance of information as wealth sink into the world's consciousness, the importance of copyright, patent, and other information protections will also turn out to be problems requiring similar international cooperation (see chapter 3).

A Higher-Stakes Game

All of these events are being played out against a background of massive shifts in the world's political structure. There are fewer and fewer dictatorships and more and more democratic regimes. At the same time that freedom is sweeping the world, old tribal values are being reasserted, and more, not fewer, nations are being formed.

This is good news for the people of the world, but it makes the practice of diplomacy and the formation of national security policy more difficult. Dealings between superpowers are a high-stakes game, but at least yesterday one knew all the players. Today, new players are being created, and doubtless more are on the way (see chapter 3).

With the whole world now tied together by an electronic infrastructure, we have what amounts to a continuous global conversation, the implications of which are similar to those of a village conversation, which is to say, enormous. In a village, there is a rough sorting out of ideas, customs, and practices over time, and news of any advantageous innovation will be shared quickly. If someone gets a raise or a favorable adjustment of his or her rights, everyone else will soon be pressing for the same treatment.

The global conversation prompts people to ask the same questions on an international scale. To deny people human rights or democratic freedoms is no longer to deny them abstractions articulated by the educated elite, but rather to prohibit customs they have seen on their television monitors. Once people are convinced that these things are possible, an enormous burden of proof falls on those who would deny them such freedoms.

Mapping Uncharted Territory

As economies change, the conventional wisdom often lags far behind reality. Thus, in today's world of rapid change, old maps and concepts of economic development will no longer help us navigate the waters of the new economy. In fact, they may prove to be as misleading as a map drawn by Gastaldi, the official mapmaker of the Venetian Republic, that showed the Strait of Anion, a body of water linking Hudson Bay with the Pacific Ocean—the so-called Northwest Passage.

Gastaldi's map was wrong, as no such body of water exists.

Nevertheless, it had a profound effect on accelerating the exploration of the North American continent; one adventurer after another sought the fabled Northwest Passage in an effort to collect the huge prize offered by the British Admiralty.

Strictly speaking, there are no economic maps to the brave new world in which we live today, so we must determine at least its general shape without them. What we do know is that intellectual capital, the driver of the new economy, can be leveraged indefinitely. Whereas fixed costs may be high, as in the production of a movie or the writing of a piece of software, the marginal cost of replication approaches zero. Increasing returns kick in; this fact, in and of itself, constitutes a huge shift in the way the world works.

Is this new economy just the same old economy with a few new twists or has there been a paradigm shift?

To a measurable extent, business strategies of the twenty-first century will be molded by the answer to this question.

CHAPTER 3

Bits, Bytes, Power, and Diplomacy

It is almost a truism that although history is made up of facts, facts do not make history. Facts, no matter how prolix, do not arrange themselves into useful knowledge. The result: some observers who look at today's world, in which the word processor has replaced the old Underwood, see only incremental change. But these observers are blind to the evidence that we are in the midst of the third-greatest revolution in human history.

By definition, a revolution causes pervasive changes in society and alters the balance of power. Old power structures crumble and new ones arise. And each of history's three greatest revolutions has been driven, to some degree, by technology.

When the principle of the lever was applied to make a plow that could turn the earth, the agricultural revolution began and the power of nomadic tribal chiefs declined. Years later, when men learned to substitute the power of water, steam, and electricity for animal muscle, the Industrial Revolution was born. Both of these massive changes took centuries to unfold. Each caused a shift in the ruling power structure.

Today, the marriage of computers and telecommunications has ushered in the information age. It has emerged with enormous speed, and the enabling factor—but not the cause—is, to a large extent, technology.

Two Cultures

Our founding fathers lived in revolutionary times, too. Theirs was a very different kind of revolution, although it was certainly no less traumatic for those living through it. They believed Thomas Paine's claim that the American Revolution marked "the birthday of a new world"[1] and was not just a battle for home rule. The Revolution was, Paine proclaimed, a way to "begin the world all over again."[2]

The founding fathers exhibited a keen interest in technology. Indeed, provision for copyright and patent protection was written into the Constitution itself. This provision was implemented by an act of Congress in 1790 that created a patent board consisting of the secretary of state, the secretary of war, and the U.S. attorney general. It was a prestigious group: Thomas Jefferson, Henry Knox, and Edmund Randolf. That board is long gone, and indeed the schism between the diplomat and the scientist has grown wider over the years. At the

---

1. Thomas Paine, *Common Sense*, 1776 (repr., New York: Penguin Classics, 1982), 43.
2. Ibid., 31.

same time, it is becoming increasingly important that the two disciplines understand each other.

Today, a significant amount of change is driven by technology, and the task of mastering these new forces is made more complex by the difficulty of communicating across disciplines. Diplomats trained in the humanities often tend to validate C. P. Snow's famous lecture "The Two Cultures," in which he argued that not only do scientists not communicate with humanists and vice versa, but also they are ignorant of each other's knowledge and appear content to stay that way.[3]

In a somewhat similar fashion, many diplomatic historians have tended to minimize or even ignore the impact of scientific discoveries on the course of history. Indeed, the indexes of many standard texts on diplomatic history do not even include the words "technology" or "economics."

Few would deny, however, that the politics of the world changed dramatically in the predawn chill on July 16, 1945, near Alamogordo, New Mexico, when the first atomic bomb exploded. Suddenly, old power relationships were changed and military doctrines had to be reexamined. Indeed, the world has not been the same since.

Little more than a decade later, on October 4, 1957, the world was jolted again by the news that the Soviet Union had launched *Sputnik*. Dr. Edward Teller, often referred to as the "father of the hydrogen bomb," lamented that the United States had lost a battle more important and greater than Pearl Harbor. President Dwight D. Eisenhower was unperturbed,

---

3. C. P. Snow, *The Two Cultures* (Cambridge: Cambridge University Press, 1998).

however. He said that the satellite itself did not raise his apprehensions one iota. In this instance, the scientist was more perceptive than the politician because the technological breakthrough of *Sputnik*, combined with the invention of the microprocessor, has dramatically affected our lives in ways that are still unfolding.

Taken together, all of these inventions have been the major enabling force in producing a massive paradigm shift in our political and economic landscape. "The key to paradigm shifts is the collapse of formerly pivotal scarcities, the rise of new forms of abundance, and the onset of new scarcities," George Gilder writes. "Successful innovators use these new forms of abundance to redress the emergent shortages."[4]

This shift is an ongoing process, and, unlike the great revolutions of the past that played out largely unseen by the vast majority of the world's population, we are all bearing witness.

Transcending the Familiar

Technology has demolished time and distance. Instead of validating Orwell's vision of Big Brother watching the citizen, just the reverse has happened: the citizen is watching Big Brother. And the beneficial virus of freedom, for which there is no antidote, is spread to the four corners of the earth by myriad electronic networks.

Nevertheless, some experts do not accept the extent of the rapid and dramatic change that is occurring today. By defini-

---

4. George Gilder, "Over the Paradigm Cliff," *Forbes ASAP* (February 1997): 29.

tion, an expert is a person with great knowledge about a legacy system (as, obviously, there can be no experts on the future). This being so, it is not surprising that despite the overwhelming evidence that we are bearing witness to a real revolution, many experts refuse to acknowledge that revolution's existence. This reaction is grounded in human nature, which has remained unchanged over the years.

When new technology becomes the enabling factor that fundamentally changes the way the world works, the experts' expertise is suddenly in danger of obsolescence. Often they denigrate the importance of change because it may threaten not only their reputation but also even their livelihood. Henry Kissinger described this phenomenon more diplomatically: "Most foreign policies that history has marked highly, in whatever country, have been originated by leaders who were opposed by experts. It is, after all, the responsibility of the expert to operate the familiar and that of the leader to transcend it."[5]

Examples abound. In the midst of World War I, an aide-de-camp to British Field Marshal Douglas Haig, after seeing a tank demonstration, opined, "The idea that cavalry will be replaced by these iron coaches is absurd. It is little short of treasonous."[6]

In our country, the ridicule and court martial of Brigadier General Billy Mitchell in the 1920s when he postulated the

---

5. Henry Kissinger, *Years of Upheaval* (Boston: Little, Brown and Co., 1982), 445.

6. Christopher Cerf and Victor Navasky, *The Experts Speak: The Definitive Compendium of Authoritative Misinformation* (New York: Pantheon Books, 1984), 244.

importance of air power by offering to sink a battleship is instructive. The secretary of war, Newton D. Baker, thought so little of the idea that he said, "I'm willing to stand on the bridge of a battleship while that nitwit [Mitchell] tries to hit it from the air."[7]

It is not hard to find similar statements from legacy experts about everything from oil supplies to school choice.

A Powerful Lever

Although the essence of sovereignty is the power to exclude others from interfering in one's internal affairs, the concept is rapidly eroding. It reaches its ultimate end point when sovereign governments call in outsiders to validate their own elections.

The Council of Freely Elected Heads of Government, headed by former President Jimmy Carter, has traveled to Panama, where the group denounced voter fraud by General Noriega; to Nicaragua, where they validated an election; and so on around the world to governments seeking international approval. Such actions must have political science philosophers such as Jean Bodin and Thomas Hobbes turning in their graves.

We also see the daily intrusion of the media into all kinds of negotiations. For example, when Anwar Sadat made his historic trip to Jerusalem, he invited Barbara Walters, Walter Cronkite, and the late John Chancellor to come along, but

---

7. Ibid., 246.

left his wife at home. He understood with great clarity that in today's world one must marshal both domestic and foreign opinion to achieve national goals.

Increasingly, one sees heads of state performing that role, as when the U.S. president and the British prime minister created public support first for Mikhail Gorbachev, next for Boris Yeltsin, and then, early on at least, for Vladimir Putin. Indeed, we constantly see actions by governments and interest groups across borders that are of the same nature as those that got Citizen Genêt, French emissary to the United States, in such trouble with George Washington.

Perhaps the most startling event of our time is the breakup of the Soviet Union. The explosion of information technology played a huge part in this drama, as documented so completely by Gladys Ganley in her book *Unglued Empire*.[8] We have the witness of former Secretary of State George Shultz, corroborated by historian Marshall Goldman, that when Ronald Reagan envisioned the use of the microchip to build a system that came to be called "Star Wars," the leaders of the Soviet Union realized they could not compete with the United States without modern technology, which their system could not produce. Shultz said, "The Soviets were genuinely alarmed by the prospect of American science 'turned on' and venturing into the realm of space defenses. The Strategic Defense Initiative in fact proved to be the ultimate bargaining chip."[9]

---

8. Gladys D. Ganley, *Unglued Empire: The Soviet Experience with Communications Technologies* (New York: Ablex Publishing Corp., 1996).
9. George P. Shultz, *Turmoil and Triumph: My Years As Secretary of State* (New York: Charles Scribner's Sons, 1993), 264.

Michael Rothschild echoed Shultz's words: "To argue otherwise was to suggest that nineteenth-century France could have remained a European power without adopting the steam engine invented in England. The profound economic and military consequences of the microchip—a technology far too complex and fast moving for the Soviet system—forced the hand of the Soviet elite."[10]

It was the first time in history that a technology not yet in existence, and ridiculed by many, furnished a powerful lever to change the world.

A Global Conversation

The magnitude of the change that information technology has wrought is breathtaking.

The contrast in the way statesmen communicate, for example, is illustrated by the fact that when Woodrow Wilson went to Paris to negotiate the Treaty of Versailles he ordered his postmaster general, Albert Burleson, to assume control over all transatlantic cable lines in order to censor the news from Europe. Today, such an action would be an exercise in futility, as no one individual or nation can block the flow of information across national borders.

Years later, in the midst of the Gulf War, Saddam Hussein proposed what was viewed in Washington as a phony peace settlement. The problem for President George H. W. Bush was how to convey that judgment to the twenty-six nations of the

---

10. Michael Rothschild, *Bionomics: Economy As Ecosystem* (New York: Henry Holt & Company, 1995), 106.

international coalition fighting Saddam. As his press secretary, Marlin Fitzwater, remembers: "The quickest and most effective way was CNN because all countries in the world had it and were watching it on a real-time basis . . . and 20 minutes after we got the proposal . . . I went on national television . . . to tell the twenty-six members . . . that the war was continuing."[11]

In this and in many other instances, the elite foreign policy establishment was bypassed. No highly trained foreign service officer meticulously drafted a note, no secretary of state signed it, and no American ambassadors called on foreign ministers to deliver the message. In the midst of a war, we entrusted a vital diplomatic message to a private television company seen by the whole world.

The contrast between then and now could hardly be more striking. Wilson's strategy was to control the flow of information by fiat. Bush realized that he had to be a winner in the world information market.

Rapid communication made possible by the convergence of computers and telecommunications has made us, ready or not, into a global community. For the first time in history, rich and poor, city dweller and peasant, north and south, east and west are linked together in a global electronic network of shared images in real time in which time zones often become more important than borders.

Information technology creates a global conversation; indeed, the Internet carries real conversations in which infor-

---

11. Debra G. Hernandez, "From Insider to Outsider," *Editor & Publisher* (December 7, 1996): 11.

mation is exchanged by millions of people on countless bulletin boards without regard to race, gender, or color. The implications of this global conversation are enormous.

On the way to his first inauguration, Abraham Lincoln expressed the sentiment that our Declaration of Independence not only gave liberty to the people of this country but also gave hope to all the world for all future time. When Lincoln made that statement, his words were heard by only a handful of people. Today, this hope is the subject of the global conversation; it prompts people to ask the same question on a global scale. In the past, the educated elite could read about democracy or capitalist prosperity. But hearing or reading of such things is not at all the same as having them happen in your village to people you can see and hear—people just a few streets or broadcast frequencies away.

As pointed out earlier, in a global village, denying people human rights or democratic freedoms no longer means denying them abstractions they have never experienced. It hardly matters that only a minority of the world's people enjoy such freedoms or the prosperity that goes with them. Once people are convinced that these things are possible, denying them these rights becomes very difficult.

The shift to an information-based economy sparked by global conversation has had a profound effect on the way nations behave. For example, when natural resources were the dominant factor of production, the conquest and control of territory seemed a reliable way to enhance national power. As recently as World War II, armies fought and men died for control of the iron and steel in the Ruhr Basin because ownership of those assets conferred real economic and political power. Today, these assets have lost their strategic value.

In the industrial age, plants became ever larger and less easy to move. Indeed, as long as capital consisted largely of factories, heavy equipment, and raw materials, there was little fear that these assets could or would move away, so the governments of the world held all the cards.

In the new economy, intellectual capital has become the dominant means of production, and it is highly mobile; it can and does move easily when the hand of government becomes too heavy or grasping.

Money has always gone where it was wanted and stayed where it was well treated. It flees onerous restrictions and heavy-handed regulation. This truism applies to both the old and the new economies, but it is even more important in the new economy dominated by information; there is nothing more easily portable than intellectual capital, which can walk, run, or fly across borders as if they did not exist.

In the industrial economy, it was common wisdom that direct labor—the people on the shop floor who produced the goods—was the most productive. The indirect labor of the technical and professional worker tended to be thought of as overhead.

Today, information technology permits just-in-time inventory with direct shipments from supplier to store in response to signals created by the cash registers at the store's checkout counter. This same technology enables custom manufacturing on a mass basis of everything from men's suits to automobiles. The huge databases recording the individual preferences of customers permit what has been called "marketing to one."[12] In this sense alone, the new economy of today is, in fact, truly new.

In the industrial economy, if you advanced the idea of making your company rich by pricing your product at zero and giving it away for nothing, you would earn very few promotions. In the new economy, this tactic has created a whole new group of millionaires. For example, Netscape gave away the first 40 million copies of its software, Sun gave away its Java language, and both companies have prospered by establishing a standard, then selling upgrades or enhancements. Every newspaper we open carries an ad for a free, or nearly free, cellular phone or a free piece of software to open an on-line bank account—all done in the valid expectation of making money on the future service to be provided. It is fair to say that this phenomenon is a function of the information/network economy that was rarely present in the industrial age.

A Giant Voting Machine

Our information-based revolution, as noted earlier in this book, is profoundly threatening to the power structures of the world, and with good reason. The nature and power of the sovereign state are being altered and even compromised in fundamental ways. The geopolitical map of the world is being redrawn. The balance of power that has prevailed for the last forty years has already been permanently disturbed and may

---

12. Don Peppers and Martha Rogers, *The One to One Future* (New York: Currency Doubleday, 1993).

soon be irretrievably altered or lost, affecting every aspect of government activity.

Much economic theory based on national markets is rendered suspect by the reality of a global market. In the world's financial markets, sovereign governments have lost control of their ability to influence the price others will pay for their currency on any but a momentary basis.

The economy has become a giant voting machine that records in real time the judgment of traders all over the world about our diplomatic, fiscal, and monetary policies. It has created what I call the Information Standard, which is far more draconian than the old gold standard and operates more swiftly.

For example, moments after a U.S. president makes a policy statement about the economy in the Rose Garden, the market's judgment of that statement is reflected in the price of the dollar. When I started in the banking business in 1946, the total foreign exchange market in New York was only about $50 million. If the Federal Reserve called Citibank or Morgan and instructed them to sell $10 million, the order could move the market. Today, we have a trillion-dollar market, and central bank intervention becomes an expensive exercise in futility.

Information Dominance

The information revolution's flood of real-time data has had a transforming effect on economic fundamentals. The substitution of information for physical capital makes this age fundamentally different from the industrial society. This phenomenon is in evidence everywhere.

Today in America, millions of square feet of warehouse space are no longer needed and have been closed because information technology has connected individual stores directly to suppliers. At checkout counters, cash registers not only record receipts, but also maintain a running inventory control. When the supply of a certain product gets low, a light goes on at the supplier's factory and trucks roll directly to the store. The interim step of stocking a warehouse and waiting for the store manager to call has been eliminated.

The changing perception of what constitutes an asset also poses huge problems for expanding or even maintaining the power of government. Unlike land or an industrial plant, information resources are not bound to a particular geography, nor are they easily taxed and controlled by government. In an economy dominated by products that consist largely of information, this power fades rapidly.

Such changes affect not only the civilian production machine on which our economic strength rests but also our military capabilities. In science, there used to be basically two ways to proceed: the first was to construct a theory and the second was to conduct experiments. Today, we have a third: computer simulation. In both Iraq wars, for example, young, basically inexperienced Americans went up against soldiers of the feared Republican Guard and beat them. A retired colonel asked one commander, "How do you account for your dramatic success, when not a single officer or man in your entire outfit ever had combat experience . . . ?" "But we *were* experienced," said the commander. "We had fought such engagements six times before in complete battle simulation at the

National Training Center and in Germany."[13] Indeed, the military today is a spectacular example of the fact that information has replaced physical assets.

Information, to be sure, has always been a vital part of any commander's strength. Where is the enemy located? How many troops are involved? How are they armed? This kind of information has often made the difference between victory and defeat. Now military intelligence is much more complex. It even has a new name: Information Dominance. Today, Apache helicopters flying over Bosnia uplink their detailed pictures of action on the ground to a satellite, record them with a video camera, or beam them directly to local headquarters. Videos taken from the air verify the Dayton Accord. Major General William Nash observed that in Bosnia, "We don't have arguments. We hand them pictures, and they move their tanks."[14]

This is a long, long way from 1943, when analysts hunted through the stacks of the Library of Congress for maps and photographs of possible German targets for Allied bombers, as few, if any, such maps and photographs existed in the war department.

"The substitution of massive information for massive firepower also lies behind the development of Battlestar, the operations command headquarters at Eagle Base," notes writer Richard Rapaport.[15] Today, even the ground troops on patrol are equipped with night-vision goggles and handheld global

---

13. Kevin Kelly, *Out of Control: The Rise of Neo-Biological Civilization* (New York: Addison-Wesley Publishing Co., 1994), 246.

14. Richard Rapaport, *Forbes ASAP* (October 7, 1996): 125.

15. Ibid.

positioning system devices to pinpoint their exact position on the ground using satellites. Because the soil is strewn with mines, knowing exactly where you are is often a matter of life and death. Mines that have been located by an airborne mine-detection system are exploded by drone Panther tanks, which are remotely controlled. So in the military, as in civilian life, information in all its forms is augmenting hard assets.

Dangerous Downsides

Our reliance on information technology and the remarkable things that can be achieved by using it has dangerous downsides as well. For example, our information infrastructures, in the words of a 1996 report of the Defense Science Board Task Force on Information Warfare, are "vulnerable to attack" and create "a tunnel of vulnerability previously unrealized in the history of conflict."[16]

We in the United States are, in the words of Owen Harries, senior fellow at the Centre for Independent Studies, "enemy deprived" in the sense that the former Soviet Union was defeated in the Cold War and we can no longer concentrate our efforts on a single major adversary. But there are many rogue states and groups that, even though they command no huge military establishment, can nevertheless conduct information warfare.

---

16. Defense Science Board Task Force on Information Warfare, *Report of the Defense Science Board Task Force on Information Warfare* (November 1996): 8.

Today we are experiencing guerrilla warfare, ethnic con-
flicts, and active terrorist groups, not unlike the Middle Ages
when soldiers fought for individual warlords. As the Defense
Science Board Task Force noted, "Offensive information warfare is attractive to many because it is cheap in relation to the
cost of developing, maintaining, and using advanced military
capabilities. It may cost little to suborn an insider, create false
information, manipulate information, or launch malicious
logic-based weapons against an information system connected
to the globally shared telecommunications infrastructure. The
latter is particularly attractive; the latest information on how
to exploit many of the design attributes and security flaws of
commercial computer software is freely available on the Internet."[17]

Such adversaries, both real and potential, have a lot to work
with because the Department of Defense has more than 2 million computers, more than 10,000 local area networks, and
more than 100 long-distance networks that coordinate and
implement every element of its mission, from weapons design
to battlefield management. During the calendar year 1995, up
to 200,000 intrusions were made into the Department of Defense's unclassified computer. These intruders "modified, stole
and destroyed data and software and shut down computers
and networks."[18]

As we've already seen, technology has irretrievably altered
the way nations communicate with each other. The channels

---

17. Ibid., 23.
18. Ibid., 35.

through which diplomatic messages move used to run from government to government, and the entrance and exit points were guarded by the foreign ministers. Now these channels are more and more being bypassed by special interest groups of all kinds, ranging from terrorists to human rights activists, until, as Andrew Arno of the East-West Communications Institute puts it, " . . . it is often more a matter of strained relations between centers of interest than whole countries."[19] We have seen these forces at work from South Africa to Korea as one pressure group after another steps around national governments to further its own crusade.

At the end of the day, effective diplomacy at critical junctures in any age is backed by the knowledge that if all else fails, military force can be used to attain national goals. Therefore, vulnerability to an attack on our information infrastructure is something that should attract serious attention.

All of this puts pressure on our national security team to master these forces that have been set loose in the world. In the absence of a visible threat to our vital national interest, attention tends to be focused elsewhere, but this would be a mistake. It is more important than ever that our foreign policy be grounded on American national interest. The new technology will not go away; it will only get better in accordance with Moore's Law, which postulates that microchips will double in density and speed every eighteen months. Bandwidth

---

19. Andrew Arno and Wimal Dissanayake, "The News Media As Third Parties in National and International Conflict," in *The News Media in National and International Conflict* (New York: Westview Press, 1984), 237.

will grow even faster. All of this has had and continues to have a profound effect on both national and international politics.

As governments could once partially control the value of their currency, they could also to some extent control what their citizens could see and hear. Today, however, sovereign states have totally lost this ability.

The entire political process is magnified, and sometimes distorted, by the images that cross our television screens. When the reporting of international events was restricted to the printed word, each of us had to create an image of an actual event in our mind. This mental process has a very different impact than, for example, seeing in real time the sad, solemn spectacle of Gulf War body bags being unloaded at Dover Air Force Base—images that have had an immediate and profound effect on the American appetite for foreign adventures.

The parade of such images has also had a profound effect on foreign policy agendas, and, as with certain wonder drugs, it has produced some negative side effects. One downside is that real-time pictures, particularly those of violent events, tend to destroy the benefit of detachment and scholarly contemplation and put pressure on policy makers to take actions that may not be fully thought out. As the distinguished editor and journalist Michael J. O'Neill put it, "It mobilizes public emotions, influences government policies, and even shapes the events themselves."[20]

---

20. Michael J. O'Neill, *Terrorist Spectaculars: Should TV Coverage Be Curbed?* (New York: Priority Press Publications, 1986), 2.

Legal Questions

Knowledge, at one time a kind of ornament to be displayed by the rich and powerful at conferences, is now combined with management skills to produce wealth. The vast expansion of knowledge has brought with it a huge increase in our ability to manipulate matter, increasing its value by the power of the mind and generating new products and substances unhinted at in nature and undreamed of only a few years ago.

Contrary to the doomsayers who postulated that the world would run out of resources by the year 2000,[21] it is difficult, if not impossible, to find a single commodity that is worth more in real terms today than it was ten years ago.

In the past, when the method of creating wealth changed, old power structures lost influence, new ones arose, and every facet of society was affected. The beginning of that process is already apparent in this third great revolution, and one can postulate that in the next few decades the attraction and management of intellectual capital will be the decisive factor in determining which institutions and nations will survive and prosper and which will not. This has created new uncertainties about copyright laws, the right to privacy, and ownership of information.

British copyright law dates back to the Statute of Anne, enacted in 1709 at a time when the only way to communicate was with pen and paper. Reformulating a concept and a law three centuries old to fit tomorrow's world is a huge challenge.

---

21. Donella H. Meadows, *The Limits to Growth* (New York: Signet, 1972).

As in most things, there are competing values to contend with.

The right of a person to own the intellectual property he or she created is enshrined in our patent and copyright laws. But in our connected world, the theft of intellectual property has become easier and constitutes a growing problem.

The rights granted by the First Amendment of our Constitution sometimes seem to conflict more and more with our right to privacy. This issue is further confused by the fact that some people want privacy while others prefer all the publicity they can get. Some want their views to get wide circulation while others wish to keep their secrets, be it the formula for Coca-Cola or the source code in a new piece of software.

All of this is complicated by the fact that today all products of the mind—from music and literature to science and mathematics—can be reduced to zeros and ones in the digital age and sent around the world at near the speed of light. The sheer volume of this digital data causes many to estimate that, in the very early years of this millennium, voice communication across the world networks will constitute less than 2 percent of the total traffic; all the rest will be data. Anne Branscomb has written that "we have not yet ventured upon a coherent effort to rationalize the legal infrastructure of the information age."[22]

Technology has usually far outstripped the law, and we have the witness of no less a legal personage than Oliver Wendell

---

22. Anne Wells Branscomb, *Who Owns Information?* (New York: Basic Books, 1994), 185.

Holmes, who pointed out in a speech at Harvard Law School that "it cannot be helped, it is as it should be, that the law is behind the times . . . as law embodies beliefs that have triumphed in the battle of ideas and then have translated themselves into action. While there is still doubt, while opposite convictions still keep a battle front against each other, the time for law has not come; the notion destined to prevail is not yet entitled to the field."[23]

The whole structure of the Internet and which law will prevail is up in the air, or, more precisely, in cyberspace. Privacy clashes on a minute-to-minute basis with the flood of information. Congress attempts to impose censorship on the Internet and runs up against the First Amendment. And because the network exists in cyberspace, no one nation or authority can lay claim to it. Engineers and scientists double the capacity of transmission lines approximately every two years and have created abundance where once there was scarcity and competition where once there was monopoly. The Federal Communications Commission (FCC) can no longer cope; indeed, Peter Huber has suggested that it be abolished as an artifact of the past. In its place he would put "nothing grander than common law. . . . The telecosm is too large, too heterogeneous, too turbulent, too creatively chaotic to be governed wholesale from the top down." In a great understatement, he goes on to say, "This is, of course, unsettling."[24]

---

23. Oliver Wendell Holmes, *Collected Legal Papers* (New York: Harcourt, Brace and Co., 1920), 291.

24. Peter W. Huber, *Law and Disorder in Cyberspace: Abolish the FCC and Let Common Law Rule the Telecosm* (New York: Oxford University Press, 1997), 206.

Patenting the Invisible

Volumes have been written about the wisdom of our founding fathers in constructing a constitution that has lasted longer than any other written constitution in history. What generally has not been acknowledged is that they understood that the odds against success of any kind in our society are formidable because no one knows what ventures in an endless stream of innovation and enterprise will be successful. In what passed for industrial policy then, they sought to promote entrepreneurship by federally granted patents. In the words of the Constitution, "The Congress shall have the power to promote the progress of science and useful arts by securing for . . . authors and inventors the exclusive right to their respective writings and discoveries."

As noted earlier, this section of the Constitution was activated by an act of Congress in 1790 that created a patent board. As a member of the board, Thomas Jefferson observed the flow of new ideas and wrote that the patent system gave a spring to invention beyond his conception. Later, President Abraham Lincoln, who held a patent for a device to help lift boats over shoals, observed that the system added the "fuel of interest to the fire of genius."[25]

The first patent was granted on July 31, 1790, to one Samuel Hopkins for a method of making pot ashes. Since then, millions of patents have been issued. At the beginning, inventors were required to submit models of their inventions to the

---

25. Abraham Lincoln, "Second Lecture on Discoveries and Inventions," February 11, 1859, reprinted in *Collected Works of Abraham Lincoln*, vol. 3 (Piscataway, NJ: Rutgers University Press, 1990), 363.

patent office. Space became scarce as the models piled up. Then a fire in the mid–nineteenth century destroyed most of them, and the practice was discontinued.

Today the patent office is overwhelmed by requests to patent things you can neither see nor touch: bits, bytes, gnomes, molecules, proteins, and combinations thereof. The progression has now reached the point at which patents are being issued for "business processes," a new and highly controversial practice that has touched off heated debate.

The U.S. Patent and Trademark Office (PTO) has had to transition from inspecting mechanical things to reviewing things unseen and has begun to issue patents on software. The issuance of patents perceived as overly broad sparked controversy and government hearings, which, in the end, caused the PTO to reverse itself on a patent granted to *Compton's New Media* on a CD-ROM search.

Although thousands of software patents are granted each year, the debate has moved to the practice of filing for business process patents, such as Amazon.com's process of "one-click ordering" and Priceline.com's business model.

On July 23, 1998, a U.S. Appeals Court validated a business practice patent held by the Signature Financial Group concerning a way of calculating mutual fund shares, which the State Street Bank in Boston had been using. Since the system enabled mutual funds to pool their assets in a single portfolio, thus producing some cost and tax savings, the ruling could create the principle that both investment strategies and trading practices can be patented.

Until this ruling, there was debate and controversy about the validity of the patent Merrill Lynch had received in 1982 for its cash-management account practice. Partly as a result of this ruling, the PTO was inundated with new applications. As patent requests had already been rising at double-digit rates, this put added pressure on the examiners. There are now business practice think tanks dreaming up new, or purportedly new, ways of doing business. Jay Walker has created just such an intellectual incubator, Walker Digital, which is busy filing a string of business process patents.

Indeed, Wall Street now puts a value on patents held by companies. The release of news that a company has been granted a patent on some piece of software or a business practice can cause the company's stock to soar.

There is little agreement on how the PTO should function in the information/network economy, but there is a steady drumbeat of discontent driving the political process to find a way to improve the system and bring it into the digital age. Not everyone is happy about this development. Although the staff of the PTO valiantly tries to keep up with the flow, they are overwhelmed by thousands of requests, some valid and some not, from people trying to cash in on the currency of the new economy.

It is said that there are many "trash" patents issued that do not truly represent unique new ideas and may be exploited by unscrupulous people to blackmail companies that fear the huge cost of lawsuits. Greg Aharonian has created a kind of one-man cottage industry denouncing the flow of trash patents, which he calls "crappy" patents. He publishes a newsletter that addresses the problem of what in the trade is called "prior art," which refers to an idea that someone else has thought of first. The search for something like software can be arduous and time consuming, so it is sometimes easy to miss a prior idea.

These patent activities are simply further illustrations of how the Internet really has changed everything.

Collocation

As the worth of data and information has escalated with the advent of the information/network economy, the search for a secure place to store this intellectual capital has intensified.

In his book *Cryptonomicon*, science-fiction writer Neal Stephenson postulated a vault on an island where the world could store its data free from the reach of governments of nation-states.[26] In an example of life imitating art, a Mr. Roy Bates and his family and associates, who run a business called HavenCo Limited, are trying to turn Stephenson's idea into a reality in an old 6,000-square-foot gunnery platform located in the North Sea some six miles off the coast of England. They have converted the platform, abandoned by the British after World War II, into what they describe as a new independent nation where data in any form can be stored free from the prying eyes of all governments and competitors. Vast amounts of computer storage will be lodged in the hollow legs supporting the facility.

HavenCo Limited's business plan is for the platform to house huge computers and redundant power supplies, all in a

---

26. Neal Stephenson, *Cryptonomicon* (New York: Avon Eos Books, 1999).

secure environment. Because a company's data is so important in the new economy, the idea of a secure home for its information is already big business in such places as California's Silicon Valley. HavenCo Limited aims to make its island platform the most secure place yet for companies to store their data.

When Bates took over this little artificial island in 1967, he declared it an independent country, named it Sealand, and appointed himself "Prince." Of course, this is not the first time someone has tried to establish a new nation on some remote island that was believed or hoped to be unclaimed by any state. The legal status of Sealand is vague at best, and obviously it could not stand up against an armed assault, but so far its former occupiers, the British, have left it alone. That, of course, is no guarantee of its future.

Win or lose, the concept of collocation—to protect the lifeblood of the modern corporation, which is data—will not go away anytime soon. Whether that data will be stored at Sealand is an open question. What is certain, however, is that everywhere the concept of privacy competes with the desire of Big Brother to learn one's secrets.

All governments hate secrecy, and often, in the name of national security, they spend large amounts of time and money to read other people's mail and prevent private citizens from using high-security codes and ciphers. In the end, it is a losing game because more and more people are able to create new ciphers of a complexity that makes it both difficult and expensive in time and money to break them.

Wisdom Sorely Needed

Science, despite all of its advances and the ways in which it is changing the world, does not remake the human mind or alter the power of the human spirit. There is still no substitute for courage and leadership.

What has changed dramatically is the explosive increase in the information available to our policy makers in coping with this new world. It is hoped that data processed by the minds of trained diplomats will produce real knowledge, and, with enough experience, even wisdom. Wisdom has always been in short supply, but it will be sorely needed in the days and years ahead because, in the words of a former president, "Only people can solve problems people create."[27]

27. Richard Nixon, 1999: *Victory Without War* (New York: Simon & Schuster, 1988), 16.

CHAPTER 4

New Rules: Different in Kind, Not Degree

The air is so full of data, both true and untrue, that it is increasingly hard to separate fact from fiction about the new knowledge-based economy. Despite this exceptional difficulty, if we are to survive and prosper in this millennium, it is crucial to make the distinction. Although each generation regards this dilemma as a new problem, it is as old as recorded history.

In one of his most famous allegories, Plato told the story of a cave where people were chained up and could only look in one direction. They could see only the shadows on the wall and could never look out at the real world beyond the cave's entrance to see what was happening. When they finally were unchained and could look out into the sunlight, they did not believe what they saw.

In some ways we are in a similar situation today. We see the shadows of an industrial society to which we are accustomed while just beyond our vision there is a fast-developing new economy that is as different from the industrial economy as was the industrial economy from the agricultural economy that preceded it.

Because change is unsettling, most of us understandably prefer the familiar; the shadows on the walls of our caves seem comfortable and real. This may be why generations of economists have honed rules for a familiar industrial economy and are understandably loath to acknowledge that a fundamental change has occurred. The celebrated science-fiction writer William Gibson has noted that the future is already here; it is just unevenly divided.[1] I would add to this that the future is unevenly divided not only among various parts of the world, but also between those who believe that there really is a new economy responding to new rules and those who do not.

Stateless Capital

It is fair to say that no economy has ever behaved in a totally predictable manner; otherwise, the pundits would not be wrong so often. The new economy is even more unpredictable than the old industrial one because it is like an ecosystem that responds to seemingly trivial events often weeks after they occur. It is for this reason that the talking heads on television who explain why the market went up 20 points or down 200 points add nothing to our economic thinking—but much to the art of creative writing.

Although this view of the new economy as an ecosystem has not gained wide acceptance among mainline economists,

---

1. William Gibson, interview by Brooke Gladstone, *Talk of the Nation*, NPR, November 30, 1999.

it nevertheless makes a great deal of sense. The natural world runs itself, and not always to the taste of some environmentalists, for many species die and disappear as new ones appear.

Similarly, with no central planning, a global capital market has emerged—the Eurodollar market—which represents the greatest floating pool of capital in the history of the world. It is a totally new phenomenon with profound implications for both nation-states and business.

Because there is a limited amount of capital in the world and an unlimited number of projects looking for finance, capital goes where it is wanted and stays where it is well treated, as noted earlier. It flees restrictive laws and regulations. This new "stateless capital" operates in real time, relentlessly seeking the best blend of safety and return. Thus it is often criticized by those who long for a process that is more orderly and predictable.

Control of Currency

The financial market of our new economic world is not a geographical location to be found on a map; it is more than 200,000 electronic monitors in trading rooms all over the world that are linked by new technology. The result is that no one is in control—or rather, that *everyone* is in control, but through collective valuations.

Until very recently, governments retained substantial power to manipulate the value of their currencies. But as the information revolution has rendered borders porous to huge volumes of high-speed information, that task has now become difficult, if not impossible.

The control of currency has always given a government great leverage over the most crucial material endeavors of its citizens. The regulation of money markets is the regulation of a society's resources in their most convenient and fungible form.

Today, the value of any currency is determined by the price that the market will pay for it in exchange for some other currency. Whatever the price, it is almost constantly being condemned by someone somewhere as too high and by someone somewhere else as too low. Few governments are entirely satisfied with the value the market places on their currency. Someone is always demanding that government do something to push the value of its currency up or down, depending on how one's interests are affected.

The power to control the price other countries will pay in their currency to obtain yours is now severely limited. Sovereign control over the value and trade of money has been irrevocably compromised and continues to erode under the new rules. The market is a harsh disciplinarian. When François Mitterrand became president of France in 1981, he was elected as a committed Socialist, and almost immediately, money began to flow out of the country, foreign-exchange reserves were rapidly depleted, and within six months Mitterrand had to reverse course and become pro-capitalist. That is not to say that governments can no longer influence, for better or for worse, the value of their currencies; they can and do, but their ability to readily manipulate that value in world markets is declining under the rules of the new economy. And currency values are increasingly less a power and privilege of sovereignty than a discipline on the economic policies of imprudent sovereigns.

A Ripple Effect

When you fire up your computer to buy or sell a stock or a currency today, you assume that your order will be executed and properly recorded. This was not always the case.

In January 1968, the New York Stock Exchange choked and broke down on a volume of less than 15 million shares, forcing the exchange to thereafter restrict volume by closing ninety minutes early. When that failed to solve the problem, the market was shut down completely every Wednesday. The paper-based system simply failed.

A study by the Rand Corporation estimated that in 1968, 25 percent to 40 percent of all brokers' deliveries had not been properly recorded or had not been recorded at all. As volume piled up at the end of the week, bank clerks merely stamped tickets "D.K." (don't know). And as the transfer process broke down, a ripple effect took place, forcing brokers to borrow stock or money. When the smoke finally cleared, more than 200 brokerage firms had disappeared. There were hundreds of millions of unclaimed dividends floating in the market and no way to establish ownership. The "fails," or incomplete security trades, totaled more than $4 billion. In fact, the federal government estimated that in the late 1960s there were some $400 million worth of securities that were just plain missing. Today, the evening news anchors report trading on the New York Stock Exchange as "moderate" even when 300 million shares change hands.

The transition from chaos to order required not only technology but also a total change of attitudes and laws. As usual, government was part of the problem. Although the SEC excoriated—with good reason—the industry's lack of management skill, no mention was made of a basic problem. In well-intentioned efforts to protect the consumer, state laws required physical stock certificates as evidence of ownership of shares. That meant that certificates had to be hand-carried from broker to transfer agent and back again. Once state laws were changed, many of the technical problems were solved by the Depository Trust Company (DTC), which immobilized certificates. Securities delivered to the DTC are now measured in trillions of dollars a year.

Risks are always present in these huge market volumes. But when there is a national debate over derivatives, it is useful to remember that it was the paper-based system that had the world of finance holding its breath as one major brokerage firm after another failed. Then, as now, it was systemic risk.

Rule of Increasing Returns

Today's new rule of increasing returns seems out of sync with conventional wisdom. In the past, it was thought that scarcity created value: the more that was produced of a given item, the less value it would have in the marketplace. Just the reverse is true today in our global information/network economy, in which one fax machine is worth nothing, but two fax machines are worth something, and 1,000 machines connected together create even greater value—a value that increases as more and more machines are added to the network. The same is true of networked computers.

Every day, additional examples of this new economic rule of increasing, rather than diminishing, returns present themselves. In fact, some mathematicians have proven, at least to their own satisfaction, that the value of a network increases as the square of the number of members. So in this sense, more creates more, as opposed to the old rule that value is created by scarcity.

One of the old rules that has become even more important in the new economy, albeit with a new twist, is the importance of people. For years, company newsletters have intoned that people are businesses' most valued asset. It turns out that in the new economy, the care and feeding of innovative talent are crucial because the interconnection of people produces the same kind of leverage as the interconnection of desktop computers.

Huge sales volumes are being leveraged every year from innovative ideas. And one of the difficulties to have sprung from this, both for management and for bean counters, is that the existence of innovative people who are organized in such a way as to exploit and leverage their talents cannot be discerned by studying the balance sheet.

The new economy has altered the traditional relationship of employer and employee in fundamental ways. Not many years ago, companies almost always owned the capital invested in the land their factories were built on as well as the factories themselves. The industrial worker was dependent on the company-owned machine. Today the knowledge worker owns the means of production, which is his or her own skill and knowledge. This gives the workforce a mobility that is unprece-dented and is reflected in the movement of employees between companies at volumes never before seen.

All products and services can be duplicated over time, and the progress of technology is moving at flank speed, so compa-nies today must sponsor lifelong learning as the only way to sustain a competitive advantage. And they have to use talent where they find it. Today, software written in India rides a satellite to a building site in Chicago, an accounting firm in New York, or anywhere else in the world. The writer requires no green card, no entrance visa, and no physical journey to earn his or her money.

This phenomenon constitutes a new kind of economic or-ganization and seriously changes the dynamics of how and where people can earn their money. For example, it is now possible to have full employment in some remote village even though no businesses are hiring people in that neighborhood or even in that nation.

Some Old Rules Do Still Apply

It is clear that we have a new and different economy. And this new economy has features that operate with new rules—rules that did not obtain in the old industrial economy.

That said, it is equally true that some old rules still apply. For example, although the new rule that more creates more does apply to the network economy, the old rule of scarcity still works in some instances. Witness the $9 baseball that Mark McGwire hit over the fence in St. Louis for home run number seventy. There is only one such ball—the ultimate measure of scarcity—and it sold for a small fortune. So sometimes the old rules and the new rules can and do coexist.

Another old rule that has retained its applicability is that markets go both up and down, and mass psychology still plays an important role in that fluctuation. The invisible hand that economist Adam Smith wrote about in the eighteenth century[2] still operates in the market—albeit now through a global electronic network that moves at warp speed.

The reason some of the old rules survive in this new world with its new rules is that the old ones were based not only on economic dogma but also on human nature. And human nature remains stubbornly unchanged. What Smith described as "the natural effort of every individual to better his own condition"[3] still motivates the people who drive the new economy, just as it did those who drove the old. Only the manner in which one achieves this goal has undergone a dramatic permutation.

---

2. Adam Smith, *The Wealth of Nations*, 1776 (repr., New York: Modern Library, 1994), 485.
3. Ibid., 581.

CHAPTER **5**

The Whiskey Ain't Working Anymore

In her continuing effort to further my education, my daughter recently sent me a CD called *Marty's Party*, featuring country and western singer Marty Stuart's latest ballads and wisdom. One of the songs is titled "The Whiskey Ain't Working Anymore." And as the last chords of Stuart's guitar faded away, it occurred to me that he could have been singing about businesses today, as the old slogans and nostrums so dear to the hearts of every business in days past just ain't working anymore in the new global information/network economy.

The situation is reminiscent of driving through the pouring rain while listening to some radio announcer in a windowless studio explaining that the weather today will be warm and sunny. It produces a kind of Alice-in-Wonderland effect. Technology has surpassed and subsumed just about everything in the world, yet the rhetoric remains unchanged.

As an example, for years the financial service industry has been split, with small-town banks worried about regional banks, regional banks worried about money-center banks, and domestic banks worried about foreign banks, all in an effort to protect what is usually described as their "market."

As the number of American banks shrank from the more than 30,000 in the 1920s to the 10,000 to 11,000 existing today, almost every other business in the world entered the financial service market in one way or another.

And while banks worried about each other, Merrill Lynch invented the Cash Management Account (CMA), and it now has customer assets that are approximately four times those of America's largest bank. Paine Webber and Charles Schwab are not far behind and are moving up rapidly. Let's face it: when the financial arm of General Electric earns more money than 99 percent of the banks in the world, it should be clear that banks have a problem that transcends worrying about what other banks are doing.

Today, all banks, big and small, are on the same side of the door, and the force that landed them there is technology. There is no use barring the door against newcomers because technology has lowered the barriers to entry into the financial service business. In the new global information/network economy, companies of all shapes and sizes are coming into that world.

A Market of One

There have been periods in American history when political campaigners have held out the vision of a time when the western farmer, the small-town businessman, and the individual investor would have the same access to money and credit as a Hamilton, a Morgan, or a Biddle. That time is now, but many still flog the dead horse of yesterday.

The new information technology has paradoxically made separate market segments both obsolete and, at the same time, more discrete through the convergence of computers and telecommunications. They have become obsolete because modern technology makes it possible for our competitors to be located anywhere in the world, and they have become more discrete because information technology permits, as mentioned in chapter 3, "marketing to one."

Giant data warehouses holding terabytes of information can be mined to produce highly detailed information about individual customers, giving the company that uses it a huge comparative advantage. Those who do not have or do not use this technology will be left behind in today's competitive world.

To make matters more complicated, protected market segments—whether geographical or functional—are, like national trade protectionism, a wasting force even though the concept still appears to have some appeal to political splinter groups.

Market protectionism of all kinds is slowly giving way to the rule of the consumer. As strategic thinker Ken Ohmae says, "At the cash register, you don't care about country of origin or country of residence. You don't think about employment figures or trade deficits. You don't worry about where the product was made. It does not matter to you that a 'British' sneaker by Reebok (now an American company) was made in Korea, a German sneaker by Adidas in Taiwan, or a French ski by Rossignol in Spain. What you care about is the product's quality, price, design, value, and appeal to you as a consumer."[1]

The same phenomenon is evident in the financial-service sector of the economy. A study commissioned by the Bankers' Roundtable noted: "Nonbanks, such as PC service providers and technology service companies, are using the information superhighway to insert themselves between banks and customers."[2]

Today, nearly every time we open our mail there is an offer of a new preapproved credit card issued by some nonbank entity owned by an automobile company, a retailer, a telephone company, a manufacturer, or even, on occasion, a real commercial bank. And what catches our eye is not so much the name of the company that issued it as the interest rate, the grace period, the annual fee, and how many frequent-flyer miles we can claim.

Retailers now routinely use nonbank merchant service companies; indeed, five of the ten largest are nonbank. This is not a transitory event, but rather a worldwide tide as the information revolution tells people in every corner of the world how others live.

Television and TiVo have created a revolution of rising expectations. Today, hundreds of millions of people are plugged in to the global network, and all of them who watch *CSI* or *Desperate Housewives* or whatever else are voting not only for Coke or Pepsi but also for free expression and free markets.

---

1. Kenichi Ohmae, *The Borderless World: Power and Strategy in the Interlinked Economy* (New York: HarperCollins, 1990), 3.

2. Edward Neumann, *Banking's Role in Tomorrow's Payments System: Ensuring a Role for Banks*, vol. 1. Report prepared for the Bankers' Roundtable (Washington, DC: Furash & Co., June 1994): 11.

Indira Gandhi is said to have remarked that in the Third World a revolution can be sparked when a poor peasant sees a modern refrigerator stocked with food in a television sitcom. People all over the globe see and hear how others live and work, and no one has to tell them that command and control economics do not work. The resultant shift toward democracy and free markets creates huge new potential markets.

Everything Is Converging

Just as mathematics has almost merged with physics, the financial-service business is now so interconnected to the manufacturing business that no meaningful line can be drawn between the computer software that controls the machine tool and the tool itself.

Financial services are now part of almost every business and are being offered to customers by everyone from the telephone company to 7-Eleven stores. Alliances are the order of the day.

The word "alliance" has come to encompass everything from a 500-page document to a handshake, and it often creates strange bedfellows. For example, Mercedes-Benz teamed with SMH, the maker of Swatch watches, for help in developing a car that appeals to young buyers.

Companies with old names are now doing new things, many of them in the financial arena. Everything is converging, and many believe there is now little difference between a product and a service.

Chris Meyer, director of the Center for Business Innovation, points out that LoJack is not a product that will prevent your car from being stolen, but a service in the sense that it will help retrieve your car if it is stolen because LoJack's hidden radio device signals the car's exact location to the police. "The product is simply a service waiting to happen; the service is the product in action. There are hundreds of such examples which will create all kinds of legal issues that are not yet evident," Meyer notes.[3]

The people at Microsoft and Intuit have forged more alliances than Henry Kissinger, and that trend will not only continue, it will accelerate. But the old rhetoric still rings throughout the land.

Decentralization Rather Than Centralization

We grow accustomed to modern technology so rapidly that it is hard to remember that as recently as 1966, the transatlantic cable could handle a grand total of 138 telephone conversations between all of Europe and all of North America. Thirty years later, in 1995, almost 30 million people and 20,000 businesses were signing on to the Internet, and their number was growing at an estimated 10 percent a month.

Between 1990 and 1995, the number of machines connected to the Internet was rising between five and ten times faster than the number of transistors on a chip.[4] The fact that

---

3. Stan Davis and Christopher Meyer, *Blur: The Speed of Change in the Connected Economy* (New York: Addison-Wesley Publishing Co., 1998), 20.

4. George Gilder, "The Coming Software Shift," *Forbes ASAP* (August 28, 1995): 149.

the New York Stock Exchange choked on 12-million-share days in 1968 and had to close on Wednesdays is now forgotten, as more than 200 Tandem processors stand ready to handle billion-share days.

And in this era of concern over derivatives and computer trading, we would do well to remember that it was the failure of a paper-based system that exacerbated the October 1987 crash.

In our new, networked world, refinement of current practice, whether in law or business or government, is no longer as important as innovation. We live in a world that favors decentralization over centralization. It is a world that is seeing the increasing importance of nongovernmental organizations, or NGOs, which run the gamut from the International Red Cross to the Save the Whales Foundation.

This is not a minor matter. The Union of International Associations identifies more than 30,000 international organizations, with the great majority being NGOs. These new agencies have multiple allegiances and global reach. An NGO was the driving force behind the proposed treaty banning the use of land mines in the wake of the Bosnian conflict. And the role of NGOs in international conferences from Rio to Tokyo is unprecedented. These NGOs represent neither business nor government interests; each represents its own special interest. How businesses advise their clients to deal with this new force has assumed increasing importance.

In addition to NGOs, there is another, unforeseen, tide running in the world. Many predicted the growth of world government and huge new world governance organizations that would control the way we live and work. This did not happen. Instead of great new international organizations, we see a loose coalition of bank regulators from many countries getting together to set up capital standards. These coalitions bypass the foreign offices and state departments that once guarded communications between nations. This bypassing of diplomatic channels is happening on many fronts. In the legal field, judges are building a kind of international community without the benefit of diplomats.

Anne-Marie Slaughter of Harvard Law School[5] has pointed out that "the Israeli Supreme Court and the German and Canadian constitutional courts have long researched U.S. Supreme Court precedents in reaching their own conclusions on questions like freedom of speech, privacy rights, and due process."[6]

Judges in the European Community meet together regularly, and in our part of the world, the Organization of the Supreme Courts of the Americas became functional in 1996. Like national bank regulators, these judges are producing a kind of judicial foreign policy. The development of the law for this new, networked world seems to be following the same path as other institutions. Slaughter sums it up this way: "Champions of a global rule of law have most frequently envisioned one rule for all, a unified legal system topped by a world court. The global community of law emerging from judicial networks will more likely encompass many rules of law, each established in a specific state or region. No high court would hand down definitive global rules. National courts would in-

---

5. Editor's note: Anne-Marie Slaughter is now Dean of the Woodrow Wilson School of Public and International Affairs at Princeton University.

6. Anne-Marie Slaughter, "The Real New World Order," *Foreign Affairs* (September–October 1997): 186.

teract with one another and with supranational tribunals in ways that would accommodate differences but acknowledge and reinforce common values."[7]

The ultimate test of these arrangements will be accountability to the people, as democracies will not want to put their fate in the hands of technocrats without oversight for very long. There may well be an increasing tension between the Act of State Doctrine[8] and the constitutional sanction of a treaty.

For example, in 1995, a Paraguayan man was executed by the state of Virginia despite an order by the International Court of Justice requiring the United States to take all measures at its disposal to stop the execution. Even the U.S. secretary of state weighed in, citing the Vienna Convention on Consular Relations, which required that foreigners accused of a crime be advised that they have a right to speak to their consul—an event that did not occur in this case. Prosecutors argued that this technical violation could not lead to a reprieve for a man who committed a horrible crime, and the Supreme Court, in a six-to-three ruling, let the execution proceed.[9] In an increasingly interconnected world, this case may be only a harbinger of things to come.

The reality that we are in the throes of true, massive change is hard for some people to grasp. The Euromarket is a good case in point. Even so talented a banker as the late Herman

---

7. Ibid., 189.

8. The Act of State Doctrine holds that nations are sovereign within their borders, and as such, their domestic actions may not be challenged in the courts of other nations.

9. Linda Greenhouse, "Court Weighs Execution of Foreigner," *New York Times* (April 14, 1998): sec. A14.

Abs opined early on that the Euromarket was a temporary and unwelcome phenomenon, and he kept the Deutsche Bank out of it for many years. Since there had never been anything like it in history, some failed to believe it would last, much less become the world's most liquid capital market. Indeed, the success of that market is just another illustration of the fact that the future is always unbelievable because we extrapolate what we know and are thus constantly surprised by totally new developments.

This is as true in politics as it is in business. When Ronald Reagan stood before the Berlin Wall and said to the leader of the Soviet Union, "Mr. Gorbachev, tear down this wall," he was ridiculed by the pundits because most people could not believe that such an event would ever occur. But it did.

On a more mundane level, when the first network of ATMs appeared on the streets of New York, many bankers assumed that the experiment would fail. The elderly, they said, would not use them, and young people would not like them. Customers, they predicted, would stay with the banks that did it the old-fashioned way since they had smiling tellers who knew the customers' names. They felt that the huge capital investment in systems and machines would go down the drain. What happened instead, as reported in the June 7, 1995, issue of *USA Today*, is that from 1990 to 1995, more than 40,000 tellers disappeared, and the process still continues.

Denial Syndrome

Denial of real change is true in all aspects of society, including sports.

In 1954, for example, more than fifty medical journals published articles proving to the writers' satisfaction that it was humanly impossible for a runner to break the four-minute barrier for the mile. All the stories were written just before Roger Bannister did just that. And in the year that followed, four other runners duplicated his feat.

Assessments of technological developments by experts are almost always wrong for the same reason. Even the best of them tend to make straight-line projections of what they know, failing to consider that the world has changed.

For example, in 1842, Sir George Biddell Airy, Astronomer Royal, was asked by the British government to examine Charles Babbage's analytical engine, the forerunner of the modern computer. After study, he pronounced it "worthless," causing the government to discontinue its funding of Babbage's experiment.[10]

In more modern times, one of the great pioneers in the computer world, Ken Olsen of Digital Equipment Corporation, opined at, of all places, the convention of the World Future Society in Boston in 1977, "There is no reason for any individual to have a computer in their home."[11] Yet in 1995, eighteen years later, people were buying personal computers at the rate of 50,000 every ten hours, and expenditures on computers were approximately equal to those on televisions.

Governments suffer even more from the malady of making straight-line projections. For example, the General Accounting Office's pronouncement in 1989 that the FDIC was going

---

10. Cerf and Navasky, *The Experts Speak*, 208.
11. Ibid., 209.

to have to be bailed out by taxpayers brought us high premiums and congressional investigations, but no taxpayer dollars ever joined the fund, as they were not needed.

Sometimes our tunnel vision prevents us from embracing new technology because we cannot see an application for our own business. The great historian Arnold Toynbee summed it up this way: "Familiarity is the opiate of the imagination."[12]

In my business lifetime, we have moved from a debate over whether to extend banking hours from the traditional 10 A.M. to 3 P.M., five days a week, to seven times 365—that is, seven days a week, 365 days a year, twenty-four hours a day. No one I know predicted that this would happen because we could not imagine a totally new way of doing business.

In a world moving rapidly to fiber optics, it is almost comforting to know that lawyers for the famous Bell Labs were at first unwilling to apply for a patent for their invention of the laser on the ground that it had no relevance to the telephone business. Those lawyers lived in a world of hard-wire and mechanical switches and could not imagine a world in which 1,300 miles of fiber-optic lines are laid every day.

Living in a world of branch banks and paper-based payment systems, we have to guard against falling into the same kind of trap. From working with dozens of companies, the former managing partner of McKinsey and Co., Fred Gluck, drew this lesson: "At some point experience becomes a negative value. It becomes negative for a company because it means commitment to existing plants and procedures. And it becomes nega-

---

12. Arnold J. Toynbee, *Civilization on Trial* (New York: Oxford University Press, 1948), 62.

tive for individual executives because they have succeeded by hewing to one path and can't or won't change course."[13]

Smart Cards

Over the years, the delivery of just about everything has changed. Not long ago, all big banks had large messenger departments because that was the only way to get documents from here to there. Today [1995], much of the financial delivery system involves plastic cards. In this country, Visa cards and MasterCards are ubiquitous, but smart cards have not yet been much in evidence, so it may be startling to learn that in 1994, the European manufacturers of these cards shipped 400 million of them, many to the Far East.

Smart cards are almost invisible in our country today, but it would be a mistake to underestimate their effect on the way the market will work tomorrow.[14] The Smart Card Forum, a consortium of more than 170 banks and vendors dedicated to understanding where all this is going, was created in 1993.[15] The 1996 Summer Olympics in Atlanta furnished a major step toward establishing a smart card payment infrastructure. Plans

---

13. Fred Gluck, "Taking the Mystique Out of Planning," *Across the Board* [later renamed *The Conference Board* magazine] 22, no. 7/8 (July–August 1985): 56–61.

14. Editor's note: In September 2005, the Smart Card Alliance predicted that the smart card industry would grow rapidly in North America, at a rate of nearly 28 percent for five years from the 132.2 million cards shipped in 2004.

15. Editor's note: The Smart Card Forum and the Smart Card Industry Association joined to form the Smart Card Alliance in 2001.

called for 300,000 rechargeable cards and 700,000 disposable cards in denominations of $25, $50, and $100.[16]

It is estimated that 88 percent of all monetary transactions in the United States are by cash or check, and of these, 83 percent are for less than $10.[17] This is the target market for the so-called memory or electronic purse cards that contain stored value that can be "spent" in pay phones or vending machines. When the stored value is exhausted, they are thrown away. Essentially, stored-value cards are electronic traveler's checks that can make exact change.

The "intelligent" smart card can be recharged when its value is spent. Contact smart cards must be put in a reader, whereas contactless smart cards communicate through radio waves and are in widespread use in Europe to pay tolls at roads and bridges.

Continuous Commerce

All forms of electronic banking, including smart cards, are following an experience curve not unlike that of bank credit cards, ATMs, and home banking. Once again, the U.S. bank system is but one of the players introducing smart cards.

In the early 1980s, French banks developed early chip specifications, and by 1993, there were 21 million cards with imbedded chips, used mostly for cash withdrawals. In this

---

16. Michele Marrinan, "No More Paper: Car Title Goes Electronic," *Bank Systems & Technology* (May 1995): 23.

17. Catherine Allen, "Is There a Smart Card in Your Future?" *Bankers Magazine* (January–February 1995): 39.

country, many of the electronic purse applications are being driven by nonbanks.

All of these developments have caused regulators and governments to wonder about their control of money and credit. The European system of central banks has produced an advisory report outlining a possible regulatory response to the proliferation of smart cards, and in this country, the Federal Reserve is beginning to wonder if Regulation E, the stated purpose of which is to protect consumers who engage in electronic funds transfers, is applicable.

The first congressional hearing has already been held to determine what, if anything, government should do about smart cards and cybercasts. While governments continue to study the situation, there are already several electronic banks in operation. First Virtual Holdings is ready to let network surfers effect payment for goods and services that strike their fancy in the electronic malls.[18]

The roster of electronic banks includes the joint venture of Microsoft and Visa, the Mondex subsidiary of National Westminster Bank issuing stored-value cards, DigiCash of Holland, and even 7-Eleven stores, which are now advertising stored-value telephone cards, to name just a few.

These new products, delivery systems, and marketing strategies are already having a profound effect. The law in general—and financial regulations in particular—lag far behind the reality of the global marketplace. The networks, which grew like Topsy, are a kind of electronic fourth dimension we call cyberspace, where information, money, and information

---

18. *Economist* (November 26–December 2, 1994): 21.

about money are exchanged by millions of people without regard to race, gender, or national origin.

The Internet is just one of many public and private networks, some built by banks, some by industry, and some by a combination of companies, such as the Interbank On-Line System, or IBOS.[19] There will be many more to come. In the words of Branscomb, ". . . cyberspace is a place or a universe of many places where users are making their own jurisdictional boundaries and developing their own standards of fair play and acceptable-use policies."[20]

This marketplace of the future will present public policy questions that are only now dimly emerging. The advent of the ATM, home banking on the personal computer, and the screen phone have moved banks into the new world of continuous commerce.

Banks are not alone. Today [1995], 43 percent of all corporations with sales of $1 billion or more are open twenty-four hours a day, seven days a week, 365 days a year, and the number is growing steadily.[21]

Continuous commerce is here to stay, and we all have to be part of it.

The Issuance and Control of Money

There are large public-policy issues raised by the new technology that touch upon a sovereign nation's monopoly on the

---

19. Editor's note: Today, IBOS is the acronym for International Banking-One Solution Association, an international banking alliance based in London. The IBOS system referred to here is no longer viable.

20. Branscomb, *Who Owns Information?*, 6.

21. Christian A. Christiansen, "Continuous Commerce," *I.D.C. White Paper* (1995): 3.

issuance and control of money. Over the years, mankind has used all kinds of things for money, from the immovable stones in the front yards of the citizens of Yap Island[22] to wampum to the more traditional silver and gold.

Whether it is today's paper currency or yesterday's bimetallism, the issuance and control of money has been a government monopoly for so long that we often forget that it is a relatively new phenomenon in America. For about seventy-five years, from 1838 to the start of World War I, the United States operated without a central bank, and each commercial bank issued dollar bills backed by the soundness of management, sometimes by doubtful state bonds and sometimes by specie.

States regulated entry, but not operations. The National Bank Act was passed in 1863 to make a market in the government bonds needed to finance the Civil War, but still there was no central bank. The act did require that banknotes issued by commercial banks be uniform in appearance and that they be backed by collateral consisting of U.S. Treasury securities.

As the old Civil War bonds were paid off, the currency base of the country declined some 60 percent from 1881 to 1890. Throughout this period, a debate raged about "free silver" and the ratio of the price at which the Treasury would buy gold and silver. This inflexible system led to panics and instability. The passage of the Federal Reserve Act finally gave the U.S. government a monopoly on the creation of money.

There is very little, if any, evidence that government has

---

22. See Milton Friedman, *Money Mischief: Episodes in Monetary History* (New York: Harcourt, Brace, Jovanovich, 1992), 3–7.

managed our currency values as well as did the commercial banks in pre–Federal Reserve days. Indeed, Nobel laureate F. A. Hayek puts it more strongly: "The history of government management of money has, except for a few short happy periods, been one of incessant fraud and deception."[23]

I cite this short history to show that in cyberspace, technology is creating something very close to the old American free-banking system by issuing electronic money, backed as in the free-banking period by some depository bank holding collateral in the form of Treasury securities and performing the clearing function.

Side by side with the impending growth of money in cyberspace is the explosion I've already noted of stored-value smart cards. In the nineteenth century, only banks issued dollar bills, but today every kind of company is issuing stored-value cards. If more and more firms issue cards for cash or credit, what will be the effect on the velocity of money? How will central banks form policies on the control of the money supply? How can we control counterfeiting in cyberspace? What will happen if the issuer of the card goes broke?

Like many wonder drugs, electronic tokens, including digital cash and smart cards, may have side effects, some of which could be lethal if not understood or contained. For example, since strings of digits can be copied, forgeries in cyberspace might proliferate unless a unique identification system can be built into the electronic token code.

Unfortunately, the sixteen-year-old hacker surfing the In-

23. F. A. Hayek, *The Fatal Conceit* (Chicago: University of Chicago Press, 1988), 103.

ternet is now being replaced by former KGB agents of great sophistication out to empty ATMs or move electronic money into their pockets. As all networks become tied together, these clever hackers can enter one network to get into another. The chips we use may themselves be Trojan horses that can collect and manipulate the data, as we found out the hard way in the construction of the U.S. Embassy in Moscow.

The Risks of Interconnectedness

As the world becomes increasingly interconnected, all networks are at risk. Viruses are becoming more sophisticated and more dangerous, and the firewall between a local area network (LAN) and other networks is growing harder to construct and to maintain.

As governments strive to protect their secrets and private bankers struggle to protect their networks and their money, a battle develops about how effective encryption can be. Indeed, the debate between the National Security Agency (NSA) and commercial firms on the types of ciphers that they can use still goes on. Part of that dialogue revolves around what kind of "key" may be used, since one of the important factors in code breaking is the length of the key.

The official government civilian cipher designed by IBM and in broad commercial use through the 1980s has a 56-bit key, although IBM's original suggestion was for a 128-bit key. Obviously, a shorter key makes the cryptanalyst's job easier. Many believe that if it is too short, the NSA can easily read all messages originated by U.S. commercial firms; but if it is much longer and therefore more secure, officials worry about sending the technology overseas, where it might fall into the wrong hands.

Not long ago, a French hacker cracked the encryption scheme of the new Netscape software in Europe, which, because of U.S. export rules, had to use a 40-bit key as opposed to the 128-bit key that can be used in the United States. Although it is said to have taken eight days and dozens of computers to crack this cipher, when enough money is involved, the time and hardware will be found. To unscramble the 128-bit key "would take 10-to-the-26th-power more time to breach,"[24] but governments fear the idea of citizens communicating in ways they cannot fathom.

The argument between a sovereign's desire to know and an individual's right to privacy is as old as government. It is said that English kings insisted that the postal system be owned by the government so that they could steam open envelopes in order to learn of impending treason.

This is basically no different from our government's attempt to launch the Clipper chip with the trapdoor to read electronic mail. Once again, technology is making control by the sovereign more difficult.

As the information revolution touches all aspects of our lives, codes and ciphers have now moved away from the exclusive province of governmental back-chambers to academic blackboards and commercial firms.

---

24. Jared Sandberg, "French Hacker Cracks Netscape Code, Shrugging Off U.S. Encryption Scheme," *Wall Street Journal* (August 17, 1995): B3.

Today RSA Data Security, Inc., makes available a public key that anyone on the network can copy and a private key that can read messages sent in the public key. This cipher is based on mathematical formulas that are easy to compute one way, but are said to be difficult to reverse unless one knows how they were constructed.[25] Already, a company called CyberCash holds licenses for public-key encryption technology from RSA, itself a partner in CyberCash. This is a long way from the first bank clearinghouses established in the nineteenth century to facilitate commerce.

Tomorrow's payment systems may well have instant transfers that will make the float an artifact of the past. But even as the speed of the network extinguishes float in the clearing systems, the growing use of smart cards will create float in the hands of the issuers. Today, these cards can hold from 3KB to 16KB of information and processing power.

It doesn't take much imagination to postulate that manufacturing costs will come down and computing power will go up in the future. Co-branding will become an increasingly important issue. The time will come when airlines will download tickets to your smart card by a screen phone or personal computer, and the card will be read at the gate, eliminating the paper tickets that often cause so much trouble and delay.[26]

As the world's networks become ever more interconnected, all our transactions are at risk. Like the NSA itself, some

---

25. Gina Kolata, "Scientist at Work: Leonard Adleman; Hitting the High Spots of Computer Theory," *New York Times* (December 13, 1994): sec. C10.

26. Editor's note: Mr. Wriston wrote this in 1995. The development he forecast is now in common use.

banks have their own teams of hackers whose job it is to break into the bank network. The NSA and the Department of Defense have used this technique for years, but many banking and commercial firms are now starting to imitate it. None of this will halt the growth in the use of networks, but it raises the issue of network security from what the auditors worry about to a real concern for us all.

The companies that insert themselves between you and your customer get a free ride on our backs. If the payment systems are not to become a commodity service, banks will have to build more information capacity into the systems. Banks are expected to provide liquidity and final settlement and to absorb risk, but currently they are not paid for doing so. New ways must be found to generate revenue to absorb these risks.

The financial marketplace of tomorrow is affected not only by geopolitics but also by local politics. The desire of politicians to assign tasks to institutions not primarily equipped to carry them out effectively is an old story, but it is now reaching the banking business. These experiments in social engineering almost always diminish the ability of the institution to carry out its primary task and to compete with others who are not so burdened.

Some students of the American school system, for example, measure the start of its decline from the time when politicians began to assign tasks beyond that of academic achievement to schools. They decreed that all students, even those who could not read or write, must graduate. Another goal put social diversity above learning. History teaches that when meritorious but extraneous goals are mandated by government for institutions not primarily engaged in those pursuits, everything suffers.

In order to monitor compliance with the new regulations, detailed reports are required. Recent [1992] estimates put the cost of regulatory compliance for banks at about $17.5 billion annually.[27] Whole departments had to be added to fill out the reports. In the words of one scholar, the person in charge ". . . has devoted so much time to those reports, he has actually forgotten that filling out reports is not the real goal of the office, which, if it is like most offices, is really supposed to be concerned with delivering services and making money."[28]

Banks continue to be forced down the same path. One of their principal mandates is set out in the Community Redevelopment Act. Once again, as social policy, the intent of the act—to make credit available to the community—is praiseworthy, but more trees will die making paper to print the regulations and the compliance forms than loans will be made—or repaid.

Although the Community Redevelopment Act itself is only four or five pages long, the regulations currently fill about ten times as many pages, and counting. Some 85 percent of the banks in our country have less than 100 employees. It is impossible for many of these banks to afford to hire enough lawyers to read the regulations, let alone ensure that management is in compliance. The Justice Department is now in the act,

---

27. Robert E. Litan and George G. Kaufman, *Assessing Bank Reform: FDICIA One Year Later* (Washington, DC: Brookings Institution Press, 1993), 48.

28. Raymond J. Domanico and Colman Genn, "Putting Schools First: Changing the Board of Ed's Priorities," *City Journal* (Spring 1992): 47–57.

but the law is so vague and the regulations so prolix that even large banks with platoons of high-priced legal talent will be open for bureaucratic reprimand, to say nothing of the time taken away from productive tasks. It is beginning to look like the school system all over again; if you graduate your quota, all is well, even though the diploma is a bad joke.

Assessing Risk

Banks have always been good at assessing risk because the management of risk is what the banking business is all about. When risks were local, a good memory and a few paper files would keep you out of trouble. In this new global market, however, only the skilled use of technology can bring together the myriad risks so that an informed judgment can be made. The credit risk of the borrower is now joined by market risk if a counterparty fails, operational risk if a computer goes down or software fails, and liquidity risk, cross-border risk, and other risks only now emerging. Building a system that can capture everything a customer does in real time is fast becoming a necessity.

Assessing risk is further complicated by the fact that many of the methods we use today to describe the state of the economy no longer reflect reality. Balance of trade figures are a case in point. The very concept of a trade balance is an artifact of the past. As long as capital—both human and money—can move toward opportunity, trade will not balance; indeed, one will have as little reason to desire such accounting symmetry between nations as between California and New York.

Commerce and production are increasingly transnational. Sometime in the mid-1980s, the volume of international production exceeded the volume of international trade. That is to say, the value of goods produced within a country by a foreign owner under a global strategy was greater than trade across borders. In addition, more and more products have value added in several different countries. Former Secretary of State George Shultz observed that he once saw a snapshot of a shipping label for some integrated circuits produced by an American firm that read, "Made in one or more of the following countries: Korea, Hong Kong, Malaysia, Singapore, Taiwan, Mauritius, Thailand, Indonesia, Mexico, Philippines. The exact country of origin is unknown." That label says a lot about where current trends are taking us.

Whatever the correct word is for these phenomena, "trade" certainly seems an inadequate description. In the monthly trade figures, how does one account for products whose exact country of origin is unknown? Since they do not include services, of what value are our trade figures? Indeed, more is left uncounted than is tabulated. The 500,000 foreign students in our country bring some $7 billion to $8 billion to the U.S. economy that vanishes from the statistics. Business and bank accounting have begun to suffer from similar omissions.

Banks Need Not Die

As I stated in chapter 2, it is crucial to remember that when the method of creating wealth changed in the past, old power structures crumbled and every facet of society was affected.

Despite competition from around the corner or around the world, banks need not die. There is no act of God decreeing their demise; rather, there is the stark necessity to understand and use the new electronic information and delivery systems that are emerging with enormous speed. We have the technology today to build a virtual bank, and if we do not do it, we can be sure that someone else will.

My alma mater, Citibank, advertises that it can serve customers "anywhere, anytime, any way." That is what customers, big or small, seem to want. And this is what they will get, either from the banks or from someone else. Competition no longer comes only from today's financial players but also from other industries located anywhere in the world. This trend will only grow, since in the decade ending in 1995, the world added 3 billion people to the capitalist system.

If we could accurately predict what services and products these people will generate, no one would believe the prediction any more than anyone believed that the Soviet Empire would self-destruct.

What one might at least postulate, however, is that in the next few decades the cultivation and management of intellectual capital will be the decisive factor in determining which business institutions and nations will survive and prosper and which will not.

CHAPTER 6

What Gets Measured, Gets Done

Almost from the beginning of recorded history, man has attempted to take the measure of things: the passage of time, the size of objects, the distance to some location. Indeed, some historians have suggested that the eminence of measurement must rank among the major achievements of mankind.

Measurement is so pervasive in our daily lives that we hardly notice or reflect upon how much we rely on the speedometers in our cars, the time on our watches, government figures on the gross domestic product (GDP), or an astronomer's discovery of the distance to some newly discovered star.

In the scientific world, there has been a coming together of nations to produce some standards, but this has been a long and divisive process. The modern metric system owes much to the Committee on Weights and Measures of the French Academy of Science in the late eighteenth century that was headed by the astronomer Jean Charles de Borda. The academy's basic decision was to settle on a base of ten and use that unit to derive volume and area. The length of the unit, later named the meter, was measured by a fraction of the arc of a meridian.

This pioneering work furnished the structure on which is built much of modern physical measurement. In October 1960, more than 150 years later, the General Conference on Weights and Measures met in Paris and named the metric system the International System of Units "based on the meter, unit of length; the kilogram, unit of mass; the second, unit of time; the ampere, unit of electric current; the Kelvin, degree of temperature; and the candelabrum, unit of luminous (light) intensity."[1] The system has continued to evolve as more and more nation-states adopt it. But there is no such agreement on how to measure the economy, even though we are inundated with data that purports to tell us how we are doing and furnishes the basis for government action in the economic arena.

An Idolatry of Numbers

American Enterprise Institute scholar Nicholas Eberstadt writes: "Where unshakable traditional beliefs or passing superstitions played official roles in the past, we now witness overconfidence based on a false precision. . . . Where antique despots surrendered to the temptations of numerology, the modern statesman proudly succumbs to the allure of 'quanto-phrenia'—an idolatry of numbers no less unreasoning, and no

---

1. Herbert Arthur Klein, *The Science of Measurement: A Historical Survey* (New York: Dover Publications, 1974), 24–25.

less poorly suited for promoting the commonweal, than its precursor."[2]

With the advent of the Industrial Revolution, it was necessary for man to devise some kind of record-keeping that was more sophisticated than that required for a one- or two-person farm. Merchants in those days often recorded transactions on pieces of paper that they posted on the wall. Historian Fernand Braudel tells us that the first known evidence of an accounts ledger, found in Florence, dates from 1211. By 1517, double-entry bookkeeping was in general use.[3] As economies grew and prospered, first dozens, then hundreds, and then thousands were employed in a single enterprise, and an accounting system had to be devised not only to keep track of what had happened but also to permit managers to make informed business decisions. Yet there still is no accounting system that has total global acceptability either for business or for governments.

In the United States, there are thousands of accounting rules, and they are constantly changing. On the other hand, in the physical world, when one says that something is ten meters long, all the world knows that they have received a universally accepted measure.

Economic measures are another story. When you read that the balance of payments of a country is positive or negative or that the earnings of some corporation are $450 million, there is no assurance that either number has been arrived at in a universally accepted manner. Part of the problem is that the

---

2. Nicholas Eberstadt, *The Tyranny of Numbers: Mismeasurement & Misrule* (Washington, DC: AEI Press, 1995), 2–3.

3. Braudel, *The Wheels of Commerce*, 572–3.

world changes faster than the measuring systems, and the information/network economy presents new and novel problems of measurement never before encountered. In the industrial age, output per man-hour and the counting of physical inventory did achieve a degree of precision, but in the new economy we are just at the beginning of the effort.

Measure Quality Rather Than Quantity

Measurement of knowledge workers' productivity is primitive at best and downright misleading at worst. We make judgments about the productivity of bank loan officers or insurance underwriters, but we have no real metrics in the service sector. Drucker has written that "work on the productivity of the knowledge worker has barely begun. . . . In terms of actual work on knowledge worker productivity, we are, in the year 2000, roughly where we were in the year 1900, a century ago, in terms of the productivity of the manual worker."[4]

The government figures, such as they are, cover less than 50 percent of the service workers in America. So when we read in the papers that productivity goes up or down, it does not mean very much because most Americans work in the service sector, and their productivity is either not measured at all or measured, as bankers were until late in 1999, by assuming that their productivity increase was zero and output rose only as a function of the number of employees. This method

---

4. Peter F. Drucker, *Management Challenges for the 21st Century* (New York: HarperCollins, 1999), 142.

of computing output solely on the basis of input affects about 25 percent to 30 percent of the service industry.[5]

Since knowledge workers constitute more than half of our workforce, improving their productivity is the linchpin upon which hangs the future prosperity of the nation. At the end of the day, this means we have to find metrics that measure quality rather than quantity.

Does a productive loan officer make a lot of loans and have a few defaults or does he or she make a few loans and have zero defaults? We have no agreed-upon measures. Indeed, there is a clear disconnect between what is traditionally measured and what is important.

In the public sector, some of the methodology dates back to the 1930s. When I started at Citibank as a lending officer, my boss told me always to check the published figures on freight car loadings in Chicago, as this was the best measure of how the economy was doing. At the time, it was a good metric, but today it is of little use. We all look at the numbers produced by the government but rarely ask ourselves if they reflect what is really happening. Numbers look so definitive, but in the case of the GDP, the numbers that have been produced are seriously misleading. The world simply moves faster than those who measure it.

The data published in October 1999 made some modest adjustment to new realities. Despite the fact that banks have been in the forefront in the use of computers in everything from basic bookkeeping to ATMs, the government numbers

---

5. For a full discussion, see National Research Council, *Information Technology in the Service Society* (Washington, DC: National Academy Press, 1994).

ascribed no productivity increase—zero—to banks. And this is in the face of the Clearing House Interbank Payment System, known as CHIPS, moving a trillion dollars a day with little if any increase in staff.

Old Rules Measure Yesterday

On another front, everyone from Main Street to Wall Street watches the inflation numbers. If the numbers are going up, we assume the Federal Reserve will take action. With so much riding on the veracity of the numbers, it was vital that a full review of their accuracy be instituted.

Accordingly, a Congressional Advisory Commission on the consumer price index (CPI), chaired by Michael Boskin, was formed. After study, the commission reported that the CPI overstated the change in the cost of living by about 1.1 percentage points per year. This number seems small, but compounded over time, the effects are enormous. For example, instead of falling by 13 percent, real hourly wages actually rose by 13 percent from 1973 to 1995.

With about one-third of federal budget outlays indexed to the cost of living, as are income-tax brackets, the distortion between the numbers reported and the real world is huge.[6]

Many analysts also look at a nation's savings rate to predict how its economy will unfold. For example, a low savings rate may foretell a scarcity of capital that could cramp the growth of the economy, whereas a larger rate portends ample money capital for expansion.

---

6. *Wall Street Journal* (December 5, 1996).

Many commentators have deplored the fact that Americans don't save enough money and that our savings rate is said to be low compared with that of other nations. And although the official numbers seem to confirm this story, it is the way these numbers are put together that assures this result.

Press reports on these numbers often run in juxtaposition to stories reporting that the inflow of money to mutual funds has just hit an all-time high, that the purchase of new homes (many people's principal asset) continues apace, that IRAs and 401Ks are bulging with cash, and that many corporate pension funds are overfunded. All of these events, plus the purchase of consumer durables, represent savings by Americans and constitute a direct disconnect from the official savings number that is derived by computing savings as the proportion of disposable income individuals set aside.

Measurement in the private sector is hardly any better. The industrial age that spawned our accounting rules had hard assets—things that you could touch and count, such as buildings, factories, and inventory. In the new economy, intellectual capital is far more important than money capital, but so far it goes mostly uncounted in the balance sheets of our corporations because it is largely ignored by the writers of accounting standards. Examples abound, but to cite just one, the value of patents is nowhere to be seen on our corporate balance sheets. This is not a trivial number.

The American accounting profession has now produced about 5,000 pages of accounting rules, but Robert Elliott, a partner of KPMG, pointed out, "At best, today's financial statements are an obsolete product. Relatively unchanged over the last 100 years, financial statements were designed to describe industrial-era assets: inventory, machinery, buildings, and land. Post-industrial enterprises run on intangible assets, such as information, research and development, brand equity, capacity for innovation, and human resources. . . . Yet none of these appear on the balance sheet."[7]

Today there is debate among the various accounting authorities of the world about how to handle "goodwill." One school of thought holds that it should be written off against earnings, which is another way of saying that intellectual capital or the worth of a brand name like Citibank or Coca-Cola has no value. On the other side of the debate is the marketplace, and the verdict of the market is loud and clear. Microsoft, for example, which has trivial fixed assets, has a market cap exceeding that of the big three automobile companies put together.[8] This being so, it becomes increasingly hard to argue that intellectual capital has no value.

The old guard will say that this view is just a way of measuring hot air and not real assets, even though many of the so-called real assets are rusted hulks in the scrap heaps of history while the firms based on intellectual capital, such as AOL, are propelling companies into the new economy.

As bad data produces bad results, both the public and the private sectors are in need of new metrics for a new economy. So far, there has been little progress in this direction, as there is

---

7. Robert Elliott, quoted in the Newsletter of Stan Ross Department of Accountancy of the Zicklin School of Business, Baruch College (Spring 1999).

8. Editor's note: This is still true today. On January 4, 2007, Microsoft's capital value was $294 billion, which was slightly more than three times the combined value of Ford Motor Co. ($14 billion), General Motors ($17 billion), and DaimlerChrysler ($63 billion). This is even more striking when one considers that DaimlerChrysler includes all of Daimler, not just the Chrysler that Mr. Wriston referred to.

a huge vested interest in the familiar and the known. But reality is beginning to sink in, and there are scattered efforts to come to grips with the need for new metrics.

There is no doubt that an essential factor in the Industrial Revolution was the use of accounting to permit the management of huge corporations, but the old rules measure yesterday and usually only a point in time.

Today, investors and credit grantors want, need, and can get an almost constant stream of useful information. Audited financial statements have their place in the stream of data, but the current accounting rules now prevent a company from publishing a cash-flow-per-share number, data that many managers believe is vital in running a business. As Elliott observes, "Financial statements are assembly-line Model T's when what is needed are instruments designed to client-specific management criteria and performance indicators, such as measures of customer satisfaction, product and process quality, innovation, new technology skills, and global business know-how."[9]

The pace of change is so swift that no bureaucracy, public or private, can keep up. Only now are efforts in both the public and private sectors beginning to attack the problem of metrics to measure the economy.

New Measurement Initiatives

The government has made a few modest changes in establishing a retail index to measure and take partially into account the explosion of e-commerce.

---

9. Elliott, Newsletter.

The new index, initiated in March of 2000, measures products sold on the Internet but omits services such as online brokerage and travel bookings. The complexity of attempting to measure the new economy is enormous; the players change, the rules change, and the output changes. Despite all the mergers that have taken place, there are far more players in the game than ever before. In Hoover Institution Fellow Michael Boskin's words, "Back when we had very few products being made by a small number of manufacturers, we needed a lot less detailed information, and it was easier to come by."[10]

In the private sector, there are many initiatives designed to create new metrics to measure the economy. One is a joint effort of Forbes, Ernst & Young's Center for Business Innovation, and the Wharton Research Program to create some kind of value index. With intangible assets playing such a huge role in stock valuation, research is needed to try to determine what factors are driving our current high stock values.

Although the project is in its infancy, many of the tenets of conventional wisdom are falling by the wayside. One of the leaders of the project reported, "Perhaps the most amazing result of our research is that two intangible asset categories—use of technology and customer satisfaction—had no statistical association with market value."[11]

The Sloan School of Management at the Massachusetts Institute of Technology is working to find a way to value intangible assets. The scope and pervasiveness of the problem is now becoming evident to all. As the co-chair of the effort put it,

---

10. *Wall Street Journal* (March 2, 2000): A2.
11. *Forbes ASAP* (April 2000): 142.

"Even the Coca-Colas and Disneys of the world are actually creating most of their value from assets that don't appear on their balance sheets."[12]

Another initiative in creating new measurements for business was undertaken by Professor Baruch Lev of New York University. In his scenario, he has devised a way to measure the earnings impact resulting from knowledge-based activities. Using his metrics, Professor Lev has constructed a chart showing the knowledge capital of dozens of firms derived by computing the discounted present value of future knowledge earnings.[13]

As the methodology gets refined, more and more companies will recognize that measuring knowledge capital will become even more important than measuring physical capital. This will apply to every occupation. All of the farmers growing produce and the people driving trucks and making durable goods will be supported and enveloped by the information/network revolution, so the urgency of new metrics for both the old economy and the new is manifest across the board.

Numbering Value

Accountants are far from comfortable with these new concepts. They like things that they can touch and feel and that have a clear cost that can be verified. One can count physical

---

12. Richard Boulton, quoted in "A Fact Factory for the New Economy," *Business Week* (February 7, 2000): 6.

13. For Professor Lev's chart and description of methodology, see *CFO* (February 2000): 52–62.

inventory and one can dig back through the records to find what an asset cost, but the concept of value raises huge questions because value is an intangible asset.

Banks, which like to have collateral for their loans, are increasingly faced with the dilemma of what constitutes good collateral. Some major banks, such as BT Commercial, now part of Deutsche Bank, have lent hundreds of millions of dollars to companies and taken as collateral the trade names and patents of those firms. The law has progressed to the point where banks are able to obtain a perfected security interest in these intangible assets.

This new kind of lending spawns a new kind of appraiser. Value appraisers give banks an appraisal of the value of intangible assets so that loan officers can make judgments about the size of the loans.

BT Commercial is not alone, and some of these loans are syndicated with many other banks. All of this moves such valuations from the conference rooms of think tanks to the real world of corporate finance.

Efforts to come to grips with the value of intellectual capital are not confined to the United States. The Swedish consulting firm Celemi has developed what it calls the Intangible Assets Monitor. Its approach is somewhat different, but it aims for the same result as other efforts—that is, to put a value on intangible assets.

One big Swedish insurance company, Skandia, is now using, both internally and with the public, a set of metrics they call the Business Navigator. In addition, the company now publishes a report on its intellectual capital as a supplement to its regular annual report. Because the report is still presented as a supplement rather than as part of the official report, it is not yet mainstream, but it clearly shows the way to the future of corporate accounting.

Precision Impossible

It took centuries for a universal system of measuring to evolve in the physical world. Measurement moved from using various parts of the human body, from the foot to the fingers, until the metric standard was in general use. From the late eighteenth century until the middle of the twentieth century, France was the custodian of a specially constructed bar of metal kept at zero degrees centigrade and bearing two finely engraved scratches exactly one meter apart. By 1960, a meter was defined by the wavelength of radiation produced by atoms of krypton-86.

No such precision will ever be possible in the economic world because the conditions to be measured change over time. Despite that difficulty, it is becoming increasingly evident that nations need a whole new chart of accounts and that business needs new methods to measure the new economy.

How does a national government measure capital formation when much new capital is intellectual? How does it measure the productivity of knowledge workers whose product cannot be counted on one's fingers? If it cannot do that, how can it track productivity growth? How does it track or control the money supply when the financial markets create new financial instruments faster than the regulators can keep track of them?

And if it cannot do any of these things with the relative precision of simpler times, what becomes of the great mission of modern governments: controlling and manipulating the national economy?

Even if some of these measurement problems are solved, as some surely will be, the phenomena they measure will be far more complex and difficult to manipulate than the industrial economies of old.

CHAPTER **7**

The Great Disconnect: Balance Sheets Versus Market Value

Because there may be money to be had, many attempts have been made to link one set of data or another with the market value of a given stock. There are those
who look at corporate results as revealed by generally accepted
accounting principles (GAAP), compare those stated values
with the market value, and declare that the market is a huge
bubble or even proclaim that the market suffers from "irratio-
nal exuberance."

Corporate CEOs whose corporation reports record accounting earnings sometimes watch their stock prices decline and complain that the market is totally unreasonable.
There are others who look at return on invested capital and
note that the so-called old-economy companies usually have
to invest large sums in plant and equipment, thus reducing
their return on capital, whereas some of the new-economy
companies have to invest far less and thus their return on
capital soars. There are numerous other theories, but all are

spawned by the fact that market values clearly do not appear to be based on six-month-old annual reports or even last week's 10-Qs. Something else is going on.

The Tobin Q

Some years ago Nobel Prize winner James Tobin created what came to be called the Tobin Q, in which he indicated that the best yardstick of market value was the replacement book value of a company. In short, the replacement cost of corporate assets should have an equilibrium relationship with their market value.

At the height of the industrial age, many agreed with Professor Tobin. Since his position was originally put forward, however, the world has changed, and argument can be made that the Tobin Q is no longer a relevant way to measure the reasonableness of a company's market value in the new economy. As MIT economist Robert Solow once wrote, ". . . there is a lot to be said in favor of staring at the piece of reality you are studying and asking, 'Just what is going on here?'"[1]

When unrecorded intellectual capital becomes the driving force in the economy, it is clear that book value and some of the old rules may not have the same relevance they once had. It is not unlike trying to measure the speed of a computer by the old industrial measures of pounds per square inch or revolutions per minute, both of which were valid in the machine age. Even though the world has changed, there is a nat-

---

1. Robert M. Solow, "How Did Economics Get That Way and What Way Did It Get?" *Daedalus* (Winter 1997): 39–58, 56.

ural desire to hang onto yesterday and to embrace the familiar. Although numbers look and are definitive, few people bother to look behind them to see how they are constructed.

Mixed Bag

We have a mixed bag in this country when it comes to measurements of all kinds. In the physical world, the United States has been an English island in a sea of metric measurement for years. Our corporate accounting also is different from that of other developed countries, as are our basic units of measurement.

Sometimes we use two different systems in the same sentence or on the same can of soda. We measure our soft drinks in ounces, but the nutritional information is presented in grams. Sometimes this disparity produces serious consequences.

The confusion between the kinds of metrics used in controlling the thruster of a space vehicle caused the loss of a $125 million spacecraft in September 1999 as it was approaching Mars. NASA controllers believed that the thrusters used to alter the direction of the craft were calibrated in metric newtons, whereas the builder had specified that they were calibrated in pounds. The difference was undetected for months, and when the final adjustments were made to the flight, the spacecraft veered off course by sixty miles as it approached Mars. No one knows its fate; it either crashed or is orbiting the sun.

The director of the Jet Propulsion Laboratory, which was in charge of the mission, said, "The real issue is not that the data was wrong. The real issue is that our process did not realize there was this discrepancy and correct for it."[2] That statement ranks right up there as world-class spin control.

The same could be said for a lot of accounting data: it may be correct as far as it goes, but it may miss that target of useful information by a wide margin. Indeed, I do not know a CEO who would attempt to guide his or her company's destiny based solely on the accounting numbers produced by GAAP, even though the dictionary definition of "corporate accounting" is "to recognize the factors that determine its true condition."

As I've noted earlier, in the United States there are thousands of accounting rules and they are constantly changing. In the physical world, on the other hand, when one says that something is ten meters long, all the world knows that they have received a universally accepted measure.

During the great 1980 inflation in the American economy, when the price level rose more than 12 percent, major corporations were forced to publish up to five different numbers for earnings per share (EPS). In the end, investors had a plethora of data but little or no information about the business of corporations. As inflation abated, the number of EPS calculations shrank until it reached its current level.

Matters affecting accounting have never moved very fast. About the time Columbus set sail, a monk named Luca Pacioli published a book on double-entry bookkeeping that is often credited with popularizing this practice. Even earlier, in 1458, one Benedetto Cotrugli, the Ragusan consul to Naples,

---

2. Andrew Pollack, "Missing What Didn't Add Up, NASA Subtracted an Orbiter," *New York Times* (October 1, 1999): sec. A1.

published a similar work, a second edition of which was published 100 years later. The fact that the second edition was unchanged after a century established a precedent of speed in accounting changes that is still the norm today.

Massive Disconnect

Since it has indeed taken centuries to get a generally accepted system of measurement in the physical world—and even then one that is largely ignored by many people in the United States—it seems clear that there is little hope of conforming our official accounting system to the realities of the information/network economy before the onset of the next phase of our economy.

What to do?

There is clearly a massive disconnect between corporate accounting and the value the market puts on a corporation's stock. Even if one does not believe in the efficient market theory, it is clear that the market is creating real-time values that are at odds with the conventional measures used by analysts. In this situation, Carver Mead's famous admonition to "Listen to the technology"[3] could be rephrased as "Listen to the market." And the market is saying that our current GAAP accounting, although useful, far from reflects current reality in the information/network economy.

As regulators and CPAs continue to debate new rules, it is clear from past history that if a corporate management wants

---

3. Carver Mead, quoted in "Carver Mead: The Spectacular Interview," *American Spectator* 34 (September–October 2001):68.

to get out its story about how value is being created, some kind of supplement detailing the company's intellectual capital is needed.

Since intellectual capital is the driver in the new economy, this information must be given prominence equal to that of the GAAP financials so that analysts and the public will get more of the data they need in order to make value judgments. Such tabulations will be different for each company, but they might cover some of the following points (applied here to a hypothetical corporation):

(1) Last year we filed for seventy-eight patents, had fifteen prior filings granted, and were able to license out eight patents to others, creating a stream of income of $230,000.

(2) Since constant learning is the only road to survival in this economy, we conducted 10,000 hours of training for our staff. Some 37 percent of all employees received some form of new training last year.

(3) To keep the new ideas flowing, we hired 350 new people last year. Some 62 percent of the new employees have a master's degree or its equivalent, and almost 50 percent have had prior business experience.

(4) Some 40 percent of all our products and services have been introduced during the last five years, so the output of our research and development continues to be good.

(5) So far, 60 percent of our departments have gone through the Six Sigma process, and the remaining departments will complete the process next year.

(6) Our personnel turnover rate fell to a new low.

This is just a sample of what a page might look like. Clearly, it would be expanded and tailored to specific companies.

Whatever the content of the list, one thing is clear: intellectual capital drives the new economy. It follows, then, that successful corporate managers must recognize that companies no longer face the competition in the marketplace that they have been familiar with for many years. To survive and prosper in the new economy, companies must now compete for the men and women with brains. If all the brains go to one segment of the economy, or to one company in your industry, but not to yours, then it does not really matter who your nominal competitors may be; you will already have lost the race. Corporate reports should reflect this reality.

CHAPTER 8

Politically Correct Versus Accurate Earnings

Just about everyone agrees that stock options are a form of compensation, but the problem is that no one knows what kind of compensation an option will turn out to be. It may be purely a psychological reward akin to winning the employee-of-the-year award, or it may turn out to be worth real money. The awarding of an option to an employee sends a message that the management thinks well of him or her, and so creates psychic income to the recipient.

No one can know at the time an option is issued whether or not it will ever be in the money. The only thing one knows for sure is that whatever charge to earnings that is decided upon at the time of the grant will distort the earnings statement and thus defeat the drive to make earnings more accurate.

Impossible to Compute

Congress, the media, and some investors don't seem to care how the charge is computed as long as there is a charge to earnings, even though no one knows what the correct charge, if any, should be. The reason it is impossible to compute is straightforward: no formula, governing body, or individual—not Black-Scholes, not Congress, not even the Gypsy in the window—knows what tomorrow will bring. If an option is issued at, say, $30 and the stock declines to $10 and stays there, any charge that has been made to earnings distorts that number because it eventually turns out that the option is worthless. Millions of options in corporate America have suffered this fate.

If the requirement to charge earnings for these options had been in effect at the time of their issuance, earnings that year would have been reported incorrectly, which now, in some instances, may be a criminal offense. On the other hand, the stock covered by this option may soar to $100 and really be worth something, but any guess at its value at the time of the grant will surely be wrong. No doubt the charge in this latter case would have been too small, so earnings would have been overstated.

Various Schemes

In an effort to go with the political tide without regard to the accuracy of the earnings report, various schemes are floated on how to value an option at the time it is issued. Without exception, all of these schemes will produce earnings distortion. One idea is to have two hapless merchant banks give a quote on a put on the stock ten years out. Any bank that can see that far ahead would be unique in history. If the banks are pressured to give a quote, as they may well be, they would be unwise not to make the quote as low as decently possible because they might actually have to buy the stock in the future. Since the future is unknown, the banks might take a big loss or realize a big gain, but either way, giving such a quote is not what most regulators would call prudent banking. The company booking such a number produced by the banks will receive plenty of kudos from the media, but the chance that the company will report what turns out to be the correct earnings that year is roughly the same as winning the lottery.

Other companies will use a mathematical model that is not designed for ten-year, nontradable options. The Black-Scholes model, such as it is, is designed for short-term, tradable options and rests on a series of assumptions, some about the unknowable future, which must be imputed into the model. Some of the same people worked on models that almost took Long-Term Capital Management broke and caused the Federal Reserve to organize a rescue party. Those using the model know going in that it is not designed for this purpose and are well aware that the chance of producing anything but a politically correct number is remote.

Accounting today is complicated enough without trying to book the unknowable. Both of these methods of computing the value of an option at the time of issuance may make the faddist happy, but will defeat the drive to have earnings reflect the reality of the business.

What to Do?

Is there any solid number—one that does not depend on a pseudoscientific or even a wild guess about the future—that might be used without distorting earnings?

The only number that will be known sometime in the future will be produced when the option is exercised. The difference between the option price and the market price will be a finite number. The company will receive only the amount paid for the option and not the market price, so that difference will be a real number. Skilled accountants working with this number may be able to calculate a cost to the company that should be charged to the earnings statement.

What the charge should be is yet to be determined, but at least accountants will have a solid number to work with rather than somebody's guess about the future. Instead of the distorted earnings reports produced by the current rush to charge something—anything, even if the amount turns out to be wrong—a methodology that will stand the test of common sense can undoubtedly be developed if people are really interested in producing a true earnings number instead of merely going with the current political flow.

CHAPTER 9

Global Accounting for a Global Market

n today's toxic atmosphere, politicians are racing with each other to pass new laws to "solve" the recent spate of corporate misdeeds. The fundamental American right to a presumption of innocence has been discarded by the media, and almost anyone can allege an accounting irregularity and drive the market cap of the accused company into single digits. Talking heads on television and radio and distinguished members of Congress with little or no knowledge of accounting routinely talk about "cooked books." When the president suggested that accounting decisions are not always black and white, he was attacked as if he had made an obscene statement, when in fact he was dead right.

Same Rules, Different Results

Scholars will recall that in the beginning, the Roman Empire operated with laws recorded on just twelve tablets that every schoolchild had to memorize. As laws proliferated over time, the twelve tablets grew to some 3,000 brass plates stored in the capital and read by nobody.

American accounting rules have outdone in a few years what the Romans took thirteen centuries to produce. Everybody is in on the act. The Financial Accounting Standards Board (FASB) has, at last count [2002], enshrined GAAP into three volumes comprising some 4,530 pages. Some of the FASB rules on how to book a single transaction run to more than 700 pages.

It should surprise no one that two skilled accountants looking at the booking of the same transaction and using their knowledge of the same rules may come out with two different results. It happens all the time in legal matters. Learned judges hearing the same testimony and reading the same briefs more often than not render split opinions of five-to-four or two-to-one. The media and Congress rarely castigate them for failing to agree unanimously, but in the accounting profession, a difference of opinion is often reported as if a fraud had been committed.

Congress, which suddenly has become the expert on the nearly 5,000 pages of rules governing private-sector accounting, prevents our own government from using GAAP. The reasons for this hypocrisy are clear. If the federal government used GAAP, the reported surplus in 2000 of $170 billion would have to be reported as a deficit of $580 billion.[1] Off-balance-sheet financing, à la Enron, is the rule rather than

---

1. U.S. Government Financial Report (Washington, DC: U.S. Government Printing Office, 2001).

the exception in government. While politicians touted the reduction of public debt, the General Accounting Office (GAO) was declaring that the future obligations of the government to its retirees exceeded the publicly held debt.[2] And although the mandating of a new oversight board to monitor auditors in the private sector is receiving accolades, the media and Congress ignore the federal auditors' report on the soundness of federal bookkeeping even though such an audit is required by law to be submitted to Congress by March 31.

The GAO's recent report states that, as in the four previous fiscal years, it was unable to express an opinion on the consolidated financial statements because of certain material weaknesses in internal controls and accounting and reporting issues. These conditions, the report adds, prevented the GAO from being able to provide Congress and American citizens with an opinion as to whether the consolidated financial statements are fairly stated. Such a statement in the private sector would hit the evening news and cause a congressional investigation into who cooked the books; in Washington it was greeted with profound silence.

How did we get to this point in national life? Are more laws and new pages of accounting rules the answer? Is there another way?

Alternative to Rules

Although GAAP accounting is the accepted norm in the United States (except, of course, by the government itself),

---

2. Ibid.

others overseas have slightly different ideas about how the books of corporations and governments should be kept. Since we are all the product of the environment in which we operate, this should surprise no one. With the plaintiffs' bar pouring money into the coffers of Congress and with the pressure to pass laws, the concept of a limited liability corporation, which has fueled the expansion of our economy, is in jeopardy.

The number of companies that have been destroyed by asbestos lawsuits grows every day. All of this public noise has led to an attempt to write a rule for everything.

Sir David Tweedie, the retired chairman of the International Accounting Standards Board (IASB), testified before Congress: "Companies want detailed guidance because these details eliminate uncertainties about how transactions should be structured. Auditors want specificity because these specific requirements limit the number of difficult disputes with clients and may provide a defense in litigation. Securities regulators want detailed guidance because these details are thought to be easier to enforce."[3]

And although this rationale makes logical sense on one level, it fails on another. It engenders a mind-set among accountants, auditors, and managers to ask the wrong question: "Is it legal?" instead of "Is it right?" High-priced lawyers and skilled merchant bankers can often find a way through the thicket of regulations because human ingenuity is such that it is impossible to cover every possibility.

---

3. Statement of Sir David Tweedie, Chairman, International Accounting Standards Board, before the Committee on Banking, Housing and Urban Affairs of the U.S. Senate, Washington DC (February 14, 2002).

Many years ago, James Madison foresaw the problem when he suggested in *The Federalist Papers*, "It will be of little avail to the people that laws are made by men of their choice if the laws be so voluminous that they cannot be read or so incoherent that they cannot be understood . . . that no man who knows what the law is today can guess what it will be tomorrow."[4] It can be argued that we have now arrived at that point in the accounting profession.

The alternative to this rule-based approach is one pursued by the IASB. The IASB has thirty-four standards, and instead of defining them in thousands of pages, it expresses most of them in double-digit memos. This view of the world of accounting is moving rapidly in Europe. Indeed, all companies resident in the European Union will have to be in compliance by 2005.

In the meantime in America, the FASB continues to crank out reams of paper and is falling farther and farther behind what is happening in the rest of the world. Is it not possible to have an understandable global accounting system for a global market? Sooner rather than later, the world will require it.

---

4. James Madison, *The Federalist Papers*, 1783 (New York: Signet Classics, 2003), 353.

CHAPTER **10**

Other People's Money

The hunt for scapegoats heats up at the end of every financial cycle when markets start to decline and paper profits disappear. The advent of the twenty-four-hour newsday means that any allegation of impropriety is endlessly repeated and drilled into the public's mind. America's time-honored legal presumption of innocence is forgotten. Trust is eroded as accusations of fraud multiply. Market value vanishes, and the companies brought to bankruptcy, or its brink, multiply. In the words of journalist Michael O'Neill, "Television creates impressions instead of ideas and emotions instead of thought."[1]

We are at the end of a cycle [2002]. The strains and flaws that were hidden by the good times are now beginning to appear, as they do at the end of every cycle. But there is a significant difference this time. What once were regional problems have spread around the world as local markets have

---

1. Michael O'Neill, *The Roar of the Crowd: How Television and People Power Are Changing the World* (New York: Random House, 1993).

morphed into a single global market. One individual's problem becomes everyone's problem. Maintaining trust in the integrity of the market, always essential, has become even more important.

The market has already punished miscreants without mercy, cutting market value in some cases to a few cents per share. But it has also meted out similar punishments to investors and employees who had no part in the alleged frauds.

Laws have been passed, and myriad groups, both private and official, are at work on "solutions." Doubtless these entities will put forth a string of ideas based on their political philosophies, native legal systems, corporate cultures, and regulatory structures.

The Problem

The basic problem is simple: Do the men and women who manage companies around the world have the necessary integrity? The plethora of complex accounting rules has made this basic challenge increasingly complicated.

There always have been, and always will be, people in every walk of life who shade the truth or fudge the numbers. No amount of new regulations or laws can overcome this flaw in human nature. Although corporations are now in the dock, the numbers game is not limited to them. Making things appear better than they really are or putting the best possible face on things is a common trait of mankind.

Even national governments manipulate data for political advantage or to meet some externally mandated criteria, such as the European Union's Maastricht Treaty. As noted in the previous chapter, if the U.S. government kept its books in strict accordance with GAAP, a reported surplus could become a deficit. For example, the reported surplus [in 2002] of $127 billion would really be a deficit of $515 billion. An accounting system reflecting such a wide disparity is not a very useful model for the private sector.

The great German writer Goethe said that character is formed "in the world's torment." There is now considerable torment in the corporate world. Character cannot be legislated; if it could, we would have a perfect world. Every country in the world has laws prohibiting fraudulent actions, but the deterrent effect of these laws seems highly questionable since jails around the globe are full. However, there are some things that can be done to make it harder for people to cross the line into fraudulent activity. The first lines of defense are honest law enforcement officers and effective auditors. A number of programmatic initiatives may also help.

Sunshine—The Best Disinfectant

U.S. Supreme Court Justice Louis Brandeis once observed that sunshine is the best disinfectant. His observation referred to the dark deeds of an earlier time, but it is all too true today. Yet, in so many places, it is sometimes difficult to know what exactly to bring out into the sunshine.

As noted earlier, in the United States, accounting rules issued by private sector accounting authorities fill nearly 5,000 pages, and that number is growing. In addition, there is a constant stream of new rules from the SEC. Accountants receive endless pages of updates from the FASB. Many state, and some local, rule-making bodies add thousands more. Because many of the rules are so complex—some running to hundreds of pages—honest men and women may differ in interpreting their meaning. Two skilled auditors, like two learned judges, may come up with two different conclusions on the same set of facts. In today's toxic atmosphere, however, a difference of opinion is often characterized as fraud. The only remedy is to let the sunshine of publicity shine on their positions in the same manner that both majority and minority opinions are published by the judiciary.

In the United States today, the amount of data required to be filed with the SEC grows ever larger. Sometimes vital information is concealed by the very abundance of data covering dozens of pages of fine print. Since these disclosures are written by accountants and often interpreted by lawyers, they can be mind-numbing. Few investors have the time or the inclination to plow through the data in order to extract useful information.

Outside the United States, GAAP accounting rules are often not regarded as the best, or even the correct, way to record transactions. Indeed, in London the IASB is now moving rapidly to construct what it calls "principles-based standards" that it hopes will be adopted worldwide. Unlike the FASB, which produces detailed instructions running to thousands of pages, the IASB proclaims broad principles and requires management to "do the right thing" based on the guidelines.

In a sense, it relies on the classic test of propriety: the smell test—if you are not comfortable seeing what you have done on the front page of the local newspaper, don't do it. That is still the best way to judge the booking of a transaction, and no amount of new rules will alter that simple fact. Because America is a litigious society, lawyers interpret its rules. The IASB standards are more general, resulting in less litigation.

In the best of all worlds, there would be a convergence of rules. No matter where a company was located, its balance sheet and income statement would be constructed using the same rules, and the required published information would follow common guidelines. This should be the goal for the global market, but it will not be achieved easily or quickly. The closest the planet has come to an agreement on universal measurement is the metric system, and despite its demonstrable functionality, its acceptance around the world has been painfully slow. It remains far from universal.

In Europe, where the metric system is in common use, Airbus still builds airplanes in inches and pounds. Pilots the world over (except in Russia and China) report altitude in feet and distance in nautical miles. Similarly, the dream of universal accounting standards will take time and patience because the issues are less finite and far more judgmental than meters and grams. At the end of the day, global markets require global standards. Regardless of the difficulty, it is time to overcome the existing obstacles.

Form or Substance in Corporate Boards

Much thought has been given over the years to constructing a form of corporate governance that would permit and encourage the efficient operation of corporations and at the same time act as a brake on management malfeasance. The structures are well known. The most obvious and widely used template is to have a majority of independent directors. This should not mean, as some suggest, that such directors would, by definition, have an adversarial relationship with management. Rather, it means that they are independent of management, able to question objectively specific transactions or overall corporate policy, and capable of lending their knowledge to a broad range of problems.

At the end of the day, the board's most important job is to hire or fire, as the case may be, the CEO. Every board should have a formal annual review of the CEO's performance conducted with the same rigor the CEO uses to evaluate his or her senior officers. This may take place in a private executive session that the CEO joins later to hear the verdict and discuss the specifics of the review.

Because today's global businesses are so huge and complex, it is essential that their boards be broken down into committees that can examine corporate functions in greater detail. It is now frequently proposed that someone knowledgeable in finance should chair a board's audit committee in order to assure honest accounting. This makes perfect sense, but it still does not guarantee that all will be well. In one famous case, a distinguished professor of accounting, who was also the dean of a leading business school, chaired a corporate audit committee. Despite his expertise, the committee totally missed the accounting disaster that overtook the company. This debacle underscores a fundamental fact: if the audit committee is lied to or if the management fails to reveal vital facts, the best experts in the world will not be able to detect fraudulent activity.

The same is true for independent outside auditors. However, inasmuch as they spend weeks and months at the company, they ought to be able to pick up red flags that should spur them to widen their inquiries. The old adage "You can't hit what you can't see" holds true for auditors and audit committees. This is not to say that a clever auditor can't be deceived over time.

Recently passed laws separate an accounting firm's audit function from its consulting business on the theory that auditors might be tempted to cave in to management on doubtful accounting practices in order to win lucrative consulting fees. This makes sense, but the downside is that since much of the technical expertise on arcane accounting questions resides with the consultants, the quality of the audits may actually deteriorate. Auditors with the backbone to stand up to management plus a board that will back them up are essential. Once again, we get back to character.

The truth is that a diligent audit committee of the board with the help of outside auditors is a good, but not perfect, shield against malfeasance. It is essential that the board committee meet with the outside auditors without any members of management present to enable them to bring up any problems they encounter in getting the information they need. This structure, in and of itself, would not detect fraud, but it affords a forum to comment on the competence, or lack thereof, of the CFO and the quality of the accounting decisions.

Other programmatic ideas may be helpful. For example, a

very simple banking regulation in the United States requires that all officers take a two-week vacation each year. It is very difficult, if not impossible, for an officer to keep a scam going when he or she is not there to control the data. A similar rule in the finance departments of corporations might be equally useful.

It is clear that what security analysts are paid at brokerage houses and merchant banks should not be dependent in any way on the underwriting volume of the firm. This problem is already being addressed.

Separating the job of board chairman from that of the CEO works well in some cases, yet having the two jobs reside in one person works equally well in others. The basic argument against having the chairman also function as the CEO is that he or she can then control the board agenda and thus control the board's discussion. This was particularly true before boards were organized into small committees to inspect everything from the financials to succession planning. Today, a committee chairman usually sets the committee's docket and reports the findings to the entire board whether or not they are on the formal agenda.

Some make the argument that boards are leaderless horses and a certain formal structure is necessary to assure that someone steps forward at crucial periods. Experience shows, however, that when a crisis arises, a natural leader from the board emerges. Electing a leader in advance tends to make for a two-tier entity instead of the collegial group that is required in times of stress.

Most reasonable people would argue that executive compensation in America is seriously offtrack. Directors responsible for setting salaries and benefits have been treated to a kind of ratchet approach invented by consultants that works in the following way. Consultants come into the boardroom with PowerPoint presentations that show the salaries being paid to other top executives in the same industry. The charts often make it clear that your CEO is only in the second quartile. This is unacceptable because your executive is clearly better than the executives of your competitors, so a raise is voted and justice done. The consultants then go to the next corporation, and the process is repeated over and over. No reorganization of corporate governance will make a dent in this ploy. Only people with a sense of proportion and the courage to speak out can halt this deleterious progression.

The same process pertains to granting stock options, which has exploded beyond reason. Although stockholders should, and mostly do, approve the plans, the individual grants are made by the board. The board should retain this power but must reestablish the rule of reason as to the number of options being awarded.

Today, an executive with an employment contract can often make more money by being fired for misfeasance than by continuing to work. It does not take an expert in ethics to know that this is wrong. Unfortunately, equally outlandish benefits that require scrutiny are being given to CEOs after they retire, in addition to good pensions and health care plans. Boards have also been giving officers huge loans with a wink and a promise that repayment will be waived. As the excesses grew during boom times, boards should have stopped them. The government has now done so. Obviously, the best arrangement, from the point of view of the owners of a business, is to sign no employment contracts. This puts the executive at risk: he has to do a good, honest job or he will be shown the door.

Excesses of any kind should be out of order. Once again, it gets down to the common sense of the board and the willingness of board members to stand up and be counted. Not long ago, self-appointed consumer advocates argued that company directors should hold no stock in the companies on whose boards they served. The idea was that if they held stock they were not truly independent. The wheel has come full circle. Now the clamor is not only for directors to have a meaningful stake in the company but also that they should be required to hold the stock for a stated period of time.

Obviously, we can't have it both ways. In the real world, either system will work. But the more you restrict what a director can or cannot do, the less attractive it becomes to serve on a board. Board membership already carries with it potential liabilities that lawmakers are trying to increase every day.

No one has addressed the question of where new board directors will come from if the financial rewards are small and the liabilities grow ever greater. This will become the hidden problem in all the outcry about corporate governance. Busy, qualified people will be reluctant to take on huge liabilities for modest rewards.

Many of the most glaring problems facing the American financial system have already been addressed by new laws and regulations. These include CEO certification of financial statements, stiffer penalties for fraud, creation of an oversight panel for the accounting industry, and the prohibition of accounting firms from acting as both consultant and auditor to a client.

Currently there are more than 300 fraud and misrepresentation statutes on the books. Like the multiplicity of accounting standards, the sheer number of laws tends to make people ask what is legal rather than what is right. History demonstrates that enacting more and more laws does not solve a problem; if it did, we would not be facing the current challenges.

In the corporate and financial world, it all boils down to what Howard Sheperd, former chairman of Citibank, said many years ago: One cannot do good business with bad people.

A Corporate Code of Conduct

As a major step toward regaining trust, business might create a code of principles, endorsed by chief executives, that gives the public and shareholders specific promises of actions to assure fiduciary fidelity.

Many big companies already have codes of conduct that could be used as a good starting point, then shortened and refined to produce a generic code. Companies might be invited to embrace their principles on a voluntary basis and promise to be governed by this code of conduct. This code would serve as a foundation for a renewal of trust with shareholders and the public. The idea of the corporate code of conduct could be loosely based on the concept of the Sullivan Principles, which played a role in ending apartheid in South Africa.

An initial step in this process would be the formation of a steering committee of CEOs of integrity to shape what these principles ought to be. Business leaders, with few exceptions, have been silent in defending the thousands of honest managers. They should regain their voice and take action by stating publicly what they believe in and will abide by. The code would be a signal to everyone that business leaders are willing to embrace a higher level of accountability because it is both right and practicable.

The principles, when formulated, should become a self-imposed standard and, when incorporated properly, should become part of the culture of every company that chooses to live by them. Of course, no principles by themselves will eliminate wrongdoing. But by embracing them, companies and their leaders would publicly signal their intention to listen to and live by what Lincoln once called "the better angels of our nature."[2]

A consistent monitoring system, easily understandable to both corporations and the public, might be established and paid for by a levy on each signatory, in the same manner as audit fees are currently assessed. The monitoring service (in the case of the Sullivan Principles, the monitor was Arthur D. Little) would issue a report card every year to each company and the public, which would supplement the auditor's report. One would hope the corporate code would gain its own credibility and that participation would become a recognized part of successful business practice.

In addition to dealing with issues such as transparency and governance that have captured the headlines, the corporate code of conduct would address matters that go beyond law.

---

2. Abraham Lincoln, First Inaugural Address (Washington, DC, March 4, 1861).

The code would attempt to treat transparency and other practical issues in a realistic rather than a legalistic way.

This is not to suggest that laws are not the basis of a civil society. It is to point out that laws often have unintended consequences. As time goes on, bureaucracies change the active verb "to compete" to the passive verb "to regulate." This creates a backward-looking system that is neither consumer nor business oriented, but bureaucracy oriented. Regulations often have a life of their own long after their original purpose is forgotten.

The Bottom Line

At the heart of this matter is the simple question, "Do the men and women who manage companies around the world today have the necessary integrity to make the system work?" In the vast majority of cases, the answer is a resounding "Yes," but there are always a few who poison the well. It is to these few that this section of the book is addressed in the hope that it will help restore trust in the many.

Although only a handful of corporate managers have broken trust with their constituents, the spotlight of the media has created the impression that the practices of the few are the norm of the many. A world without trust would be savage. Every interaction—from waiting for a train to drinking a glass of water—would be approached with trepidation. Trust is a universal value just as dishonesty is a universal flaw. Part of the corporate code would address integrity—its creation, development, and nurture.

Commerce must train, encourage, and cultivate good people. At the end of the day, people of integrity can make any organizational structure work well and honestly, whereas those who lack integrity can thwart any safeguards. So-called organizational ethics are dependent on personal ethics. A man's character is his fate. Excellent organizational systems of checks and balances, although useful, do not make good people. It is the other way around: Good people make good organizations. A corporate code of conduct might help this process.

AFTERWORD

by Kathryn D. Wriston

When **Walter died** of pancreatic cancer in 2005, he was described in many articles as a towering figure in American finance, and justly so. Walter was with Citibank for thirty-eight years and was chief executive officer for seventeen of those years. He was an innovator and in many ways an entrepreneur, someone willing to take a risk and venture into new areas when others were reluctant to do so. Under his leadership, Citibank developed such financial innovations as the negotiable certificate of deposit and the automated teller machine, which have become essential parts of our everyday lives, and it rapidly expanded the credit card business. The number of branches and services offered to businesses and consumers was greatly increased, both domestically and overseas. Although Walter made the bank's ultimate goal profitability rather than asset growth (which was the goal of most of its competitors), under his leadership, Citibank's assets grew 761 percent, from $17,497 billion to $150,586 billion, a remarkable increase.

Walter was a man of great character and integrity, a believer in elemental fairness. He was a champion of women and minorities in banking and in management. He was known to say, with regard to women in management, "Women have half the brains in the world—why wouldn't you use them?" He was enormously proud of Citibank and Citibankers around the world, and he was a believer in teamwork and in giving credit where and to whom due. He was intensely loyal—to his family, his friends, and the bank. He had a great sense of humor, a dry wit. At his retirement dinner from the bank, the centerpieces were festooned with knitting needles to remind us all of his rapier wit—as if we needed reminding!

A person of enormous energy and creativity, Walter was blessed with a vision of what might be, versus just being satisfied with what was, and with the dynamism and drive to get to where he was headed. He was a person who could see what something or someone might become, and he worked hard to make that happen. He was a believer in human freedom and dignity and the connection between individual freedom, free markets, and personal and economic progress.

Walter was an intellectual, although he never thought of himself as such. He was a thinker who was most at home in the realm of ideas. He was a voracious reader of everything from biographies and autobiographies—particularly of seminal figures in American and European history such as George Washington, John Adams, and Alexander Hamilton and modern-day figures such as Ronald Reagan and Margaret Thatcher—to books on history, economics, political philosophy, business, and technology. These volumes filled the libraries of his home and office, and he used them to research his articles and speeches. He also had a lighter side, which was reflected in the mystery stories, westerns, and popular fiction he read and in his love of music, particularly the big bands, Louis Armstrong, and Ella Fitzgerald.

Walter loved to write and to speak. He did so throughout his career and particularly after he retired from the bank in 1984. He was an early user of computers and the Internet and from the start saw their implications for progress and human liberty. His first book, *Risk and Other Four-Letter Words*, was published in 1986. His focus on technology and its implications was reflected in subsequent speeches and articles as well as in his second book, *The Twilight of Sovereignty: How the Information Revolution Is Transforming Our World*, which was published in 1992. In that book, he focused on the availability of uncensored information on a global scale and its implications for political, social, and business institutions—indeed, for sovereignty itself. He coined the phrase "the information revolution," and his statement "Information about money has become almost as important as money itself" is engraved on a wall of the New York Library of Science, Industry, and Business. He saw information technology as a beneficial virus, one that would promote human liberty, which, to him, was the quintessential human value.

As a financial and business person, Walter also foresaw the challenge to economic statistics, whether national, international, or corporate, that would result from the information revolution in that most of its most significant impacts are not now measured or recorded. Moreover, they are not incorporated into governmental fiscal and monetary planning on a national or international level. Current measures largely reflect the manufacturing and industrial economy that replaced the farm economy many years ago. Walter pointed out that the information/network economy applies knowledge stemming from the free and global flow of information to create value. However, the measurement itself, how to measure it, and who should establish the measures are being hotly debated as I write this. The fact that in the United States we are now experimenting with adding a measure of the value of research and development to the measurement of our gross national product is an important development that would greatly please him.

As detailed in "Notes to the Reader," Walter had prepared a manuscript reflecting the views he set forth in several of his speeches and articles from 1992, following the publication of *The Twilight of Sovereignty*, until mid-2000. The last chapter of that unpublished manuscript was on measurement. He set the manuscript aside in mid-2000 to focus more of his writing and speaking on the measurement issues that stemmed from the information revolution and the increasing importance of technology globally.

After Walter's death, as I looked through his later articles and speeches and noted their focus on measurement, I thought that what Walter would have done, had he not been stricken with cancer, would be to complete and publish the manuscript. I conferred with the other members of our family and the vote was unanimous that we do just that. Hence this book, which is being published posthumously.

This is an important book in that it carries forward Walter's views on the impact of technology globally, including the measurement issues that are now being debated. Walter was known as a thinker and innovator, someone who in many ways was ahead of his time. I think this book is another example of that.

I would like to thank our friend George P. Shultz for the thoughtful and excellent foreword he has written for inclusion in this book, as well as for the "Notes to the Reader" and footnotes he added. George and Walter were longtime friends. They met when George was serving in the Office of Management and Budget in the Nixon administration and Walter had recently become chairman and CEO of Citicorp and Citibank. They loved to discuss and debate the issues of the times and spent many interesting hours in many locations doing just that. I know that Walter would be very pleased with George's willingness to write the foreword and with the foreword itself as well as with his efforts on "Notes to the Reader" and the footnotes, and I thank him on behalf of Walter and the entire Wriston family.

I would also like to thank Charles O. Prince, chairman and CEO of Citigroup, and his colleagues, Michael E. Schlein and Nicholas Balamaci, for their invaluable assistance to me since Walter's death. Their patience and encouragement with this book is something that I will never forget, nor will I ever forget Chuck Prince's kindness to me. I know that I speak for each member of the Wriston family in expressing gratitude to them all. I am also grateful to Stephen W. Bosworth, dean of the Fletcher School of Law and Diplomacy; to Anne Sauer, the director of Archives at Tufts University; to Roger Hertog, Lawrence Mone, and Walter's many friends and colleagues at the Manhattan Institute; and to Thomas Bartos and Kurt Willett at Citigroup for their assistance and support.

I want to thank John McCarty, who has skillfully edited both Walter's original unpublished manuscript and his subsequent speeches and articles that have been added to complete this book. I am also grateful to David R. Henderson, who subsequently edited Walter's book, and Susan Southworth for her work in preparing the manuscript for publication. I know that I speak for Walter, too, in expressing my appreciation for the extraordinary efforts and support of all of these individuals.

Kathryn D. Wriston
July 2007

SELECTED BIBLIOGRAPHY

Periodicals, Papers, and Reports

Allen, Catherine. "Is There a Smart Card in Your Future?" *Bankers Magazine* (January-February 1995): 39.

Boulton, Richard. Quoted in "A Fact Factory for the New Economy." *Business Week* (February 7, 2000): 6.

CFO (February 2000): 52–62.

Christiansen, Christian A. "Continuous Commerce." *I.D.C. White Paper* (1995): 3.

Defense Science Board Task Force on Information Warfare. *Report of the Defense Science Board Task Force on Information Warfare* (November 1996).

Domanico, Raymond J., and Colman Genn. "Putting Schools First: Changing the Board of Ed's Priorities." *City Journal* (Spring 1992): 47–57.

Drucker, Peter F. "Keynes: Economics as a Magical System." *Virginia Quarterly Review* 22 (1946): 534.

Economist (November 26–December 2, 1994): 21.

Elliott, Robert. Quoted in Newsletter of Stan Ross Department of Accountancy of the Zicklin School of Business, Baruch College (Spring 1999).

Forbes ASAP (April 2000): 142.

Gibson, William. Interview with Brooke Gladstone. "Talk of the Nation." NPR (November 30, 1999).

Gilder, George. "The Coming Software Shift." *Forbes ASAP* (August 28, 1995): 149.

———. "The Emancipation of the CEO." *Chief Executive* (January–February 1988): 9.

———. "Over the Paradigm Cliff." *Forbes ASAP* (February 1997): 29.

Gluck, Fred. "Taking the Mystique Out of Planning." *Across the Board* 22, no. 7/8 (July–August 1985): 56–61.

Greenhouse, Linda. "Court Weighs Execution of Foreigner." *New York Times* (April 14, 1998): Sec. A14.

Hazard, Samuel, ed. *Hazard's Register of Pennsylvania XVI*, no. 5 (August 1, 1835): 66.

Hernandez, Debra G. "From Insider to Outsider." *Editor & Publisher* (December 7, 1996): 11.

Johnston, William B. "Global Work Force 2000: The New World Labor Market." *Harvard Business Review* (March–April 1991): 119.

Karlgaard, Rich. "Editor's Letter." *Forbes ASAP* (January 1994): 9.

Kolata, Gina. "Scientist at Work: Leonard Adleman; Hitting the High Spots of Computer Theory." *New York Times* (December 13, 1994): Sec. C10.

Lincoln, Abraham. First Inaugural Address, Washington, DC, March 4, 1861.

———. "Second Lecture on Discoveries and Inventions." In *Collected Works of Abraham Lincoln*. Vol. 3. Piscataway, NJ: Rutgers University Press, 1990.

Marrinan, Michele. "No More Paper: Car Title Goes Electronic." *Bank Systems & Technology* (May 1995): 23.

Mead, Carver. Quoted in "Carver Mead: The Spectator Interview." *American Spectator* 34 (September–October 2001):68.

Neumann, Edward. *Banking's Role in Tomorrow's Payments System: Ensuring a Role for Banks*. Vol. 1. Report prepared for the Bankers' Roundtable. Washington, DC: Furash & Co., June 1994.

Pollack, Andrew. "Missing What Didn't Add Up, NASA Subtracted an Orbiter."*New York Times* (October 1, 1999): Sec. A1.

Rapaport, Richard. *Forbes ASAP* (October 7, 1996): 125.

Sandberg, Jared. "French Hacker Cracks Netscape Code, Shrugging Off U.S. Encryption Scheme." *Wall Street Journal* (August 17, 1995): B3.

Sanford, Charles S., Jr. "Financial Markets in 2020." Paper presented at the Federal Reserve Bank of Kansas City's Symposium on "Changing Capital Markets: Implications for Monetary Policy," Jackson Hole, WY, August 20, 1993.

Slaughter, Anne-Marie. "The Real New World Order." *Foreign Affairs* (September–October 1997): 186.

Solow, Robert M. "How Did Economics Get That Way and What Way Did It Get?" *Daedalus* (Winter 1997): 39–58.

Tweedie, Sir David. Statement before the Committee on Banking, Housing and Urban Affairs of the U.S. Senate, Washington, DC, February 14, 2002.

U.S. Government Financial Report. Washington, DC: U.S. Government Printing Office, 2001.

Wall Street Journal (March 2, 2000): A2.

Wall Street Journal (December 5, 1996).

Wriston, Walter B. "Freedom and Democracy in the Information Age." *Technology in Society: An International Journal* 26, nos. 2/3, April-August 2004. © 2004 by Elsevier Scientific Publishing Company. All rights reserved. Reprinted in sections of chapters 1 and 3 by permission.

Books

Arno, Andrew, and Wimal Dissanayake. "The News Media As Third Parties in National and International Conflict," in *The News Media in National and International Conflict*. New York: Westview Press, 1984.

Arquilla, John, and David Ronfeldt. *In Athena's Camp: Preparing for Conflict in the Information Age*. Santa Monica, CA: Rand, 1997.

Branscomb, Anne Wells. *Who Owns Information?* New York: Basic Books, 1994.

Braudel, Fernand. *The Wheels of Commerce: Civilization and Capitalism, 15th–18th Century*, Vol. 2. New York: Harper & Row, 1982.

Brown, Richard D. *Knowledge Is Power: The Diffusion of Information in Early America, 1700–1865*. New York: Oxford University Press, 1989.

Cerf, Christopher, and Victor Navasky. *The Experts Speak: The Definitive Compendium of Authoritative Misinformation*. New York: Pantheon Books, 1984.

Davis, Stan, and Christopher Meyer. *Blur: The Speed of Change in the Connected Economy*. New York: Addison-Wesley Publishing Co., 1998.

Drucker, Peter F. *Management Challenges for the 21st Century.* New York: HarperCollins, 1999.

———. *The Unseen Revolution: How Pension Fund Socialism Came to America.* New York: HarperCollins, 1976.

Eberstadt, Nicholas. *The Tyranny of Numbers: Mismeasurement & Misrule.* Washington, DC: AEI Press, 1995.

Friedman, Milton. *Money Mischief: Episodes in Monetary History.* New York: Harcourt, Brace, Jovanovich, 1992.

Ganley, Gladys D. *Unglued Empire: The Soviet Experience with Communications Technologies.* New York: Ablex Publishing Corp., 1996.

Hayek, F. A. *The Fatal Conceit.* Chicago: University of Chicago Press, 1988.

Holmes, Oliver Wendell. *Collected Legal Papers.* New York: Harcourt, Brace and Co., 1920.

Huber, Peter W. *Law and Disorder in Cyberspace: Abolish the FCC and Let Common Law Rule the Telecosm.* New York: Oxford University Press, 1997.

Kelly, Kevin. *Out of Control: The Rise of Neo-Biological Civilization.* New York: Addison-Wesley Publishing Co., 1994.

Kissinger, Henry. *Years of Upheaval.* Boston: Little, Brown and Co., 1982.

Klein, Herbert Arthur. *The Science of Measurement: A Historical Survey.* New York: Dover Publications, 1974.

Litan, Robert E., and George G. Kaufman. *Assessing Bank Reform: FDICIA One Year Later.* Washington, DC: Brookings Institution Press, 1993.

Locke, John. *Two Treatises of Government.* 1689. Edited by Peter Laslett. Cambridge: Cambridge University Press, 1960.

Madison, James. *The Federalist Papers*. 1783. New York: Signet Classics, 2003.

Meadows, Donella H. *The Limits to Growth*. New York: Signet, 1972.

National Research Council. *Information Technology in the Service Society*. Washington, DC: National Academy Press, 1994.

Nixon, Richard. *1999: Victory Without War*. New York: Simon & Schuster, 1988.

Ohmae, Kenichi. *The Borderless World: Power and Strategy in the Interlinked Economy*. New York: HarperCollins, 1990.

O'Neill, Michael J. *Terrorist Spectaculars: Should TV Coverage Be Curbed?* New York: Priority Press Publications, 1986.

―――. *The Roar of the Crowd: How Television and People Power Are Changing the World*. New York: Random House, 1993.

Paine, Thomas. *Common Sense*. 1776. Reprint, New York: Penguin Classics, 1982.

Peppers, Don, and Martha Rogers. *The One to One Future*. New York: Currency Doubleday, 1993.

Quinn, James Brian. *Intelligent Enterprise: A Knowledge and Service Based Paradigm for Industry*. New York: The Free Press, 1992.

Rothschild, Michael. *Bionomics: Economy As Ecosystem*. New York: Henry Holt & Company, 1995.

Shevardnadze, Eduard A. *The Future Belongs to Freedom*. New York: The Free Press, 1991.

Shultz, George P. *Turmoil and Triumph: My Years As Secretary of State*. New York: Charles Scribner's Sons, 1993.

Smith, Adam. *The Wealth of Nations*. 1776. Reprint, New York: Modern Library, 1994.

Snow, C. P. *The Two Cultures*. Cambridge: Cambridge University Press, 1998.

Stephenson, Neal. *Cryptonomicon*. New York: Avon Eos Books, 1999.

Toffler, Alvin and Heidi. Foreword to *In Athena's Camp: Preparing for Conflict in the Information Age*, by John Arquilla and David Ronfeldt. Santa Monica, CA: Rand, 1997.

Toynbee, Arnold J. *Civilization on Trial*. New York: Oxford University Press, 1948.

Tuchman, Barbara W. *A Distant Mirror: The Calamitous 14th Century*. New York: Alfred A. Knopf, 1978.

Wriston, Walter B. *The Twilight of Sovereignty: How the Information Revolution Is Transforming Our World*. New York: Scribner Book Company, 1992.

ABOUT THE AUTHOR

Walter B. Wriston retired as chairman and chief executive officer of Citicorp and its principal subsidiary, Citibank, N.A., on September 1, 1984, after having served as chief executive officer for seventeen years and in various other positions with the company for thirty-eight years.

Mr. Wriston was born in Middletown, Connecticut, on August 3, 1919, and graduated from Wesleyan University and the Fletcher School of Law and Diplomacy at Tufts University. Following a year's service as a U.S. State Department officer and a four-year tour with the U.S. Army during World War II, Mr. Wriston joined Citibank in 1946 as a junior inspector in the Comptroller's Division.

He was assigned to the National Division in 1949 and served in the division's Canadian and Transportation districts for seven years, becoming an assistant cashier in 1950, an assistant vice president in 1952, and a vice president in 1954.

Mr. Wriston joined the bank's Overseas Division in 1956, heading the European District for three years, and was named a senior vice president in 1958. The following year he was made head of the Overseas Division and was appointed executive vice president in 1960. Mr. Wriston became president and chief executive officer of the bank in 1967 and of the corporation when it was formed in 1968. He became chairman in 1970.

Mr. Wriston was a director of the General Electric Company, the Chubb Corporation, and J.C. Penney, Inc. After his retirement from Citicorp, he served on other boards, including Bechtel Investments, Inc.; Pfizer; Sequoia Ventures, Inc.; Tandem Computers, Inc.; United Meridian Corporation; and ICOS Corporation. He was chairman of President Ronald Reagan's Economic Policy Advisory Board, a member and former chairman of the Business Council, and a former co-chairman and policy committee member of the Business Roundtable. He was a trustee of the American Enterprise Institute and of the Manhattan Institute for Policy Research, a member of the Board of Visitors of the Fletcher School of Law and Diplomacy, and a life governor of New York Hospital.

Mr. Wriston's best-selling first book, *Risk and Other Four-Letter Words*, a collection of essays, was published by Harper & Row in 1986. He followed it in 1992 with the thought-provoking and influential *The Twilight of Sovereignty: How the Information Revolution Is Transforming Our World*, published by Scribner Book Company, an imprint of Simon & Schuster.

President George W. Bush honored Mr. Wriston with the Presidential Medal of Freedom on June 23, 2004.

Mr. Wriston died in 2005, leaving behind his wife, the former Kathryn Ann Dineen, whom he married in March 1968; one daughter, Catherine; a son-in-law, Richard M. Quintal; a grandson, Christopher W. Quintal; and a granddaughter, Barbara Catherine "Katy" Quintal. His first wife, Barbara Brengle, died in 1966.

INDEX

International System of Units, 92
Internet
    financial services and, 79–80
    growth of, 9
    information/network economy
        from, 7–8
    as information superhighway, 68
    interconnected risks of, 85–86
    laws and, 49
    machines connected to, 70–71
    products sold on, 100
    revolution of, xv–xvi
Intuit, 70
inventions, 31
inventory control, cash registers
    and, 38, 41
investor class, 22

Jefferson, Thomas, 5, 19, 29, 50
Jet Propulsion Laboratory, 107–8
joint ventures, 79
judges, 72
judicial networks, 72–73

Karlgaard, Rich, 13
Kennedy, John F., 20
Keynes, John Maynard, 21
Kissinger, Henry, 32, 70
knowledge
    in information/network econ-
        omy, 16
    matter manipulated with, 13
    power of, 11–13
    wealth produced from, 47
knowledge workers
    earnings impact of, 101
    in information/network econ-
        omy, 62–63, 109–10
    productivity measurements of,
        94–96
Knox, Henry, 29

labor, 17
LAN. *See* local area networks
land ownership, 15
laws
    accounting and, 120, 128
    in civil society, 133
    copyright, 47
    enforcement officers of, 123
    human nature and, 122–23
    Internet and, 49
    judicial networks and, 72–73
    regulations and, 2–3
    of Roman Empire, 116–17
    white-collar crime punished by,
        128
learning, lifelong, 7, 63, 110–11
legacy systems, 32
legal infrastructure, 48–49
Lev, Baruch, 101
liabilities, 130–31
limited liability corporations, 119
Lincoln, Abraham, 37, 50
loans, 102
local area networks (LAN), 83
Locke, John, 2
LoJack, 70
Long-Term Capital Management,
    114

machines, 17, 70–71
Madison, James, 120
management
    directors independent of, 126
    of intellectual capital, 90
    risk, 23–24
manufacturing, 8
    financial service industry inter-
        connected with, 69
    real value created by, 16
market price, 115
market protectionism, 67–68
market segments, 67